Ashton and Mar
Trolleybuses

Bob Rowe

Picture research and additional information

John A Senior

© 2006 Venture Publications Ltd

ISBN 1905 304 13 7
ISBN 978 1905 304 134

Frontispiece

Ashton's attractive red, white and blue livery was still in use when five post-war Crossleys were delivered. Number 80 is seen here in Ashton Town Centre. *(GL)*

Facing page: Most people today who can still remember trolleybuses in Manchester will probably best recognise the Burlingham-bodied BUTs. Surprisingly perhaps, they were in fact the group of trolleybuses with the shortest lives, lasting only from 1955 to 1966. The first to arrive was No. 1302, and was the only one of the class to operate from Rochdale Road garage. It is seen towards the end of its life at Audenshaw. *(GL)*

Introduction

December 31st 2006 sees the fortieth anniversary of the final day of trolleybus operation in Manchester, which, in keeping with the events of the period, was provided by two preserved vehicles supplied by enthusiasts, the final day of public operation in Ashton and Manchester occurring on the previous day, Friday 30th December 1966. In this present World Cup Year, many people will probably remember 1966 as being the year England won the World Cup. Interestingly, 1966 was also the year in which Barclaycards were first issued and the era of shopping with plastic was born. Back in 1966, by virtue of some smart car journeys, provided by a driver who is now Chairman and Managing Director of one of the last independent bus groups in the country (and who will, therefore, will remain nameless), the writer was able to witness the final events at both Mossley Road and Hyde Road that night. Prior to that, a first visit to Manchester had been made only in 1962, so personal experience of trolleybus operation in Ashton and Manchester is limited to the last handful of years, but a wealth of information has been put at the writer's disposal, covering almost the whole of the history, to more than compensate for this omission. 1966 was also the year in which I met my wife, who grew up in Manchester close to the terminus of the Platt Lane trolleybus service, whose school was next to the Princess Road bus depot and who lived near Maine Road football ground. I therefore dedicate this book to her. Some individuals in life receive so many blessings . . .

Progress in publishing and photographic reproduction mean that images, at best forty years old, can be viewed today as good, if not better, than has ever been possible. Many photographs have never been published before, but no apology is made for using images that may, under the circumstances, not be new to the reader. In producing this volume, I have taken the opportunity to briefly review the general situation concerning trolleybus operation in the North West before looking at Ashton and Manchester in detail. I have attempted to give an historical review of developments, including some detail of the background in the country to the major decisions that were made, with illustrative coverage as appropriate. There then follows a geographic photographic section on a route basis, with finally a brief colour section.

Trolleybus operation was never destined to become as widespread as the use of trams, this assertion applying equally to the country in general as well as to the North West in particular. Whilst I have, therefore, tried to capture the flavour of a vehicle of which I have fond memories, this is most certainly not intended to be the definitive history of trolleybus operation in both locations; one day, no doubt, an author far better equipped than me will complete this task.

Ashton's trolleybuses perhaps never looked quite as distinguished in their later livery; the Peacock Blue and Primrose lacked the bolder image of the earlier Red, White and Blue livery as seen on this same vehicle on page 2. *(GLC)*

Manchester too revised its livery from Pilcher's original 'fairground livery' as applied to the prewar fleet through the tamer Neal version to the final and rather drab London Transport style seen below after economies in painting took over. *(GLC)*

In the beginning

Unlike some other areas of the country, the North West was not blessed with a multitude of trolleybus operators; nor could it count amongst its number the pioneering systems. Both Stockport and Ramsbottom, nevertheless, managed to provide services with this hybrid vehicle before the First Word War when, within five months of each other, services commenced in their respective towns in 1913. Even before this, a delegation from Manchester had inspected the German systems in Langenfeld, Ahrweiler and Mulhausen in 1908, as a result of which the Corporation decided to seek powers to operate 'omnibuses without rails powered by electric motors obtaining energy from overhead wires'. Neither the term 'trackless' nor 'trolleybus' was then in use, it will be noted. The following year the first 'trolleybus' in Britain, built by the Railless Electric Traction Company, was demonstrated to the Metropolitan Electric Tramways at its Hendon depot in September 1909. A report in Motor Traction, whilst acknowledging that it was the first in the country, stated that 'it was similar to those at Manchester', which has given rise to much speculation over the years. Perhaps they meant that it was similar to those *inspected* by Manchester, although it is known that there was a connection between the Trafford Park Estates in Manchester and the Railless Company. Furthermore, the Italian 'Filovia' type car, two of which were at one time reputed to have been ordered for Bradford, appointed Watlington & Co, who had works in Trafford Park, as their agents.

Stockport introduced its trackless services on 10th March 1913 and chose the unusual Lloyd-Kohler system, where the twin wires were suspended one above the other; only one set of wires being provided for both directions. When the vehicles met, they exchanged trolleys (apparently known locally as the 'monkey'). The route ran from St Petersgate in the town centre along Churchgate and Hall Street to Offerton Fold, the vehicles being supplied by Brush. The pioneering nature of this arrangement, and the fact that much German equipment was used, which was unobtainable from a country with whom Britain was at war, and politically unacceptable following it, led to an early end to trolleybus operation in this part of Cheshire. Final journeys were made in September 1920, making it among the first trolleybus systems to close.

Ramsbottom's contribution to transport history was multi-faceted. Very few English Urban District Councils managed to establish their own public transport operations; only this one ever ran trolleybuses, and this was largely because the tramway to which the Council aspired was beyond the financial means of such a small authority. So it was that on 14th August 1913 the first public trolleybus service in Lancashire commenced, with a route from Holcombe Brook railway station to Edenfield. The combination of solid tyres and granite setts was not conducive to the longevity of these early vehicles (a theme which will repeat itself again elsewhere), which were supplied by the previously mentioned RET Construction Company, so that within two years the original bodies were replaced. At the same time two further RET vehicles were supplied.

The first demonstration in this country of a 'trackless trolley car' took place in 1909 at the Metropolitan Electric Tramway's depot in Hendon, north London.
(GLC)

5

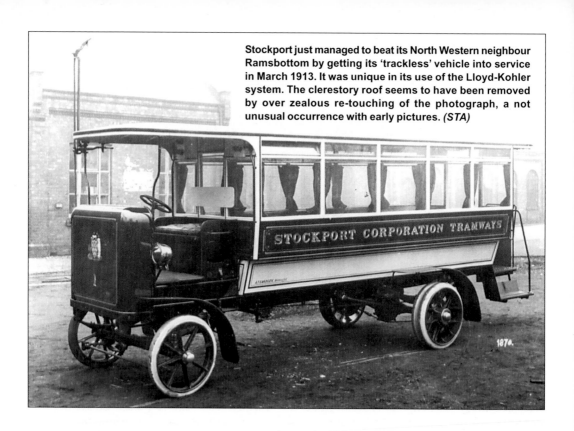

Stockport just managed to beat its North Western neighbour Ramsbottom by getting its 'trackless' vehicle into service in March 1913. It was unique in its use of the Lloyd-Kohler system. The clerestory roof seems to have been removed by over zealous re-touching of the photograph, a not unusual occurrence with early pictures. *(STA)*

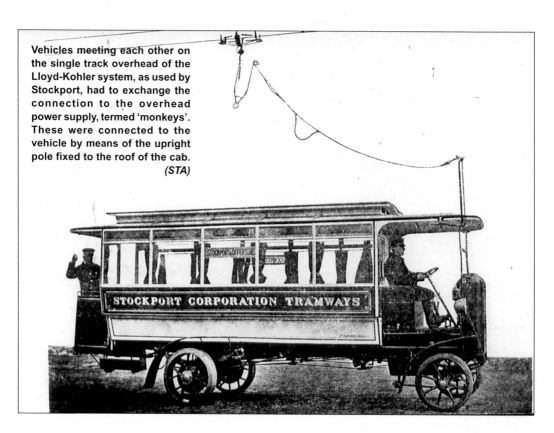

Vehicles meeting each other on the single track overhead of the Lloyd-Kohler system, as used by Stockport, had to exchange the connection to the overhead power supply, termed 'monkeys'. These were connected to the vehicle by means of the upright pole fixed to the roof of the cab. *(STA)*

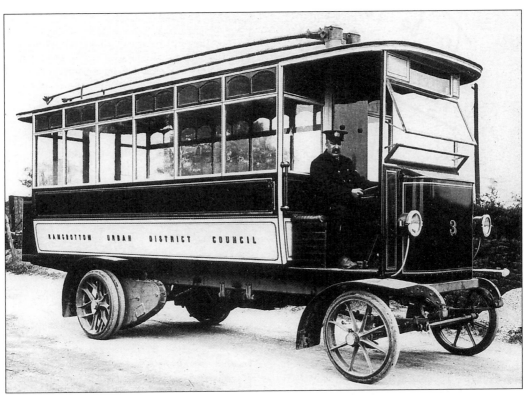

Ramsbottom received four vehicles in August 1913 which were supplied by the RET Construction Company, with bodies by Milnes Voss. The original number 3 is depicted above. Two further vehicles from RET were supplied in 1915, one of which is shown below. This pair had bodies by Lockwood & Clarkson, who were to subsequently rebody the original four trolleybuses. *(STA both)*

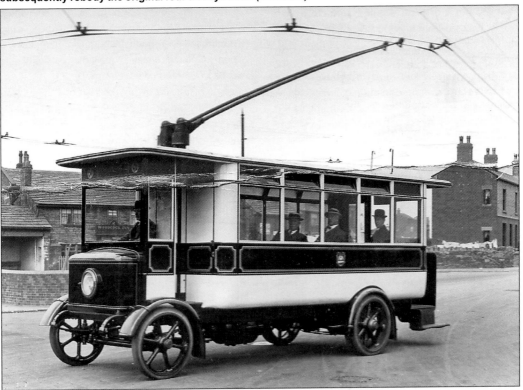

Elsewhere in Lancashire the Corporation in Wigan began operating trolleybuses in May 1925; again the system was not to be long-lived, operation finishing in 1931. In this instance the vehicles were supplied by Clough, Smith & Co, and their introduction was in part due to the fact that Wigan Corporation had inherited two tramways of different gauges. Rather than go to the expense of regauging the line to Martland Mill, trolleybuses were used. However, by 1931 Wigan's last tram had run and the trolleybuses found themselves in the strange position of having to use redundant tram overhead and track, complete with skate, to access the depot. Final journeys were made on 30th September that year.

Across the County Palatine, east of Manchester, Ashton and Oldham Corporations had, since 1921, following the acquisition of the Oldham, Ashton and Hyde Tramway Company (a BET subsidiary which had commenced operation in June 1899), operated a joint tram service between the respective towns. By 1923 this line, which was single-track with passing places, was in urgent need of renewal. The intention was to provide double tracks throughout the length of the route. However, as is frequently the case, good intentions are quite often thwarted by unforeseen circumstances. In this case, the unpredictability was the attitude of Lancashire County Council. In order to accommodate the double tracks, the bridge in Oldham Road over

the River Medlock at Bardsley, required widening. Ashton Corporation was of the opinion that since the road was a highway maintained by the County Council, the cost should be borne by them, but the County Council refused to meet the costs of bridge works to accommodate a tramway.

As a result, following the visit of a deputation to Birmingham to inspect the trolleybus system there (which had commenced in November 1922, and was the first tram to trolleybus conversion in the country), it was decided to convert the Ashton – Oldham route to trolleybus operation, a cost comparison indicating that this course of action showed savings over the provision of a double-track tramway. The fact that the Council had already purchased the rails for relaying the Oldham route does not seem to have been part of the calculation! Ten single-deck trolleybuses were ordered from Railless Limited, two of which were to be allocated to Oldham Corporation. Like many episodes in the story of the trolleybus in this part of the North West, their introduction was not, therefore, so much a positive move, but rather a response to an impasse. Thus it was to fall to the North West to witness the first example of joint trolleybus operation in this country (a feature not at all common in the 60 year history of the type, unlike the far more numerous examples provided by its antecedent, the tram), and on 26th August 1925 the Councils of Ashton and Oldham started running trolleybuses (or trackless trams, as the locals would refer to them, subsequently just shortened to 'trackless') between the two towns. This circumnavigation of the altercation by determining to replace the errant tramway with trolleybuses, was, under the circumstances, a situation where the description 'trackless' could not have been more appropriate.

Whilst Ashton seems to have entered into this new venture with some degree of enthusiasm, the same does not appear to have been the case with its neighbour Oldham, which was destined to become one of the shortest lived operators in the annals of trolleybus history. In July 1926 the General Manager of Oldham Corporation advised Mr C Irwin Baker, the Ashton Manager, that it was Oldham's intention to suspend the joint trolleybus service because so many complaints had been received that the solid-tyred vehicles were noisy and caused considerable vibrations running

Two of the new vehicles were intended for Oldham Corporation, and one of the pair is seen here just after delivery. The body was constructed by Shorts of Rochester, who were, at the time, the owners of Railless. (GLC)

over stone setts. It is believed that the volume of claims received by Oldham played no small part in this decision being reached; this in an era when today's compensation culture was unheard of! From 4th September 1926 Ashton's trolleybus service terminated at Hathershaw, and trams were reinstated between there and Oldham. This setback did not deter other authorities in the North West from investing in the trolleybus, however, for St Helens introduced their trolleybus fleet in July 1927, followed by the South Lancashire Transport Company in August 1930. For the record, it needs to be noted that Ramsbottom's system officially closed on 31st March 1930, although it is believed all trolleybuses had been withdrawn by 1928. From 21st July 1931 St Helens and SLT commenced a joint service, only the second of its kind, between St Helens and Atherton, which was to last considerably longer than the original joint operation described above.

Back in Ashton, the innovative vehicles were not without their problems, but the removal of the resistances from underneath the body to the roof, and the fitting of pneumatic tyres helped ease a lot of the trouble. In addition, the original centre-entrance bodies by Short Bros were subsequently rebuilt to rear-entrance configuration. These modifications went a considerable way to ensuring that these vehicles were to continue operating until the much larger Ashton/Manchester network had been established, of which more in due course.

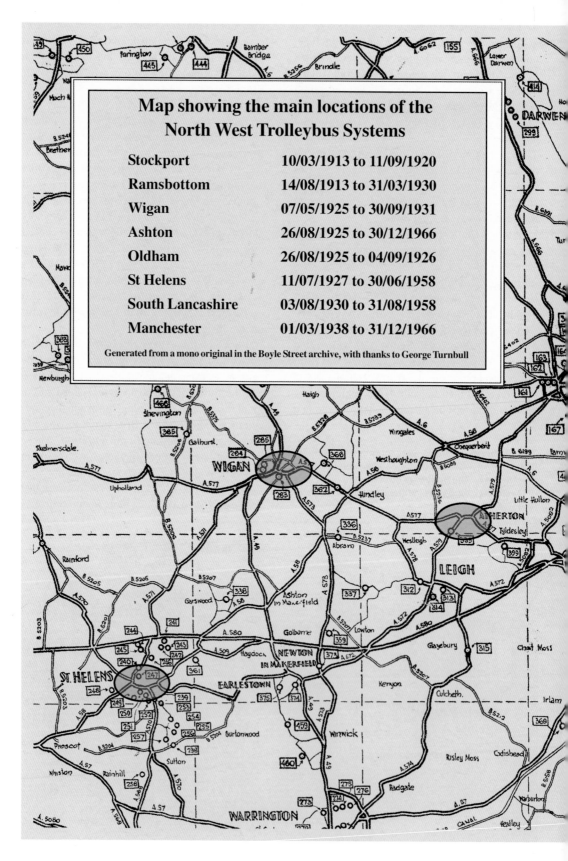

Map showing the main locations of the North West Trolleybus Systems

Stockport	10/03/1913 to 11/09/1920
Ramsbottom	14/08/1913 to 31/03/1930
Wigan	07/05/1925 to 30/09/1931
Ashton	26/08/1925 to 30/12/1966
Oldham	26/08/1925 to 04/09/1926
St Helens	11/07/1927 to 30/06/1958
South Lancashire	03/08/1930 to 31/08/1958
Manchester	01/03/1938 to 31/12/1966

Generated from a mono original in the Boyle Street archive, with thanks to George Turnbull

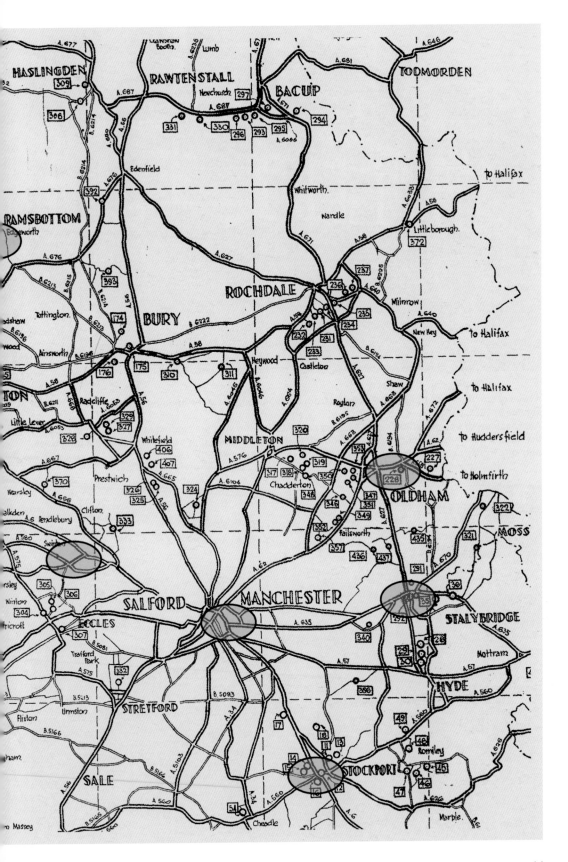

A total of ten 'trackless trams' were ordered from Railless Limited for the opening of the Ashton – Oldham service in 1925. *(STA)*

Another view of one of Ashton's new Railless cars, clearly showing the centre entrance. Later in their life the bodies were rebuilt and the entrance moved to the rear. It was using a skate trailed in the tram track, only one trolley being required to be in touch with the overhead. *(GLC)*

Six of the Railless trolleybuses delivered to inaugurate Ashton and Olham's first service were fitted with longitudinal seating as seen above; the other four had a mix of longitudinal and transverse, the seating capacities being 36 and 37 respectively. *(GLC)*

St Helens' first trolleybuses, single-deck Garretts with Ransomes bodies, were lined up outside the Town Hall, before entering service between Prescott and Nutgrove in July 1927. *(RM)*

South Lancashire Transport commenced trolleybus operation in August 1930, when ten Guy BTX six-wheel vehicles with Roe lowbridge bodies, based at the company's Platt Bridge depot, entered service between Atherton and Ashton in Makerfield. *(STA)*

Crossley

FAMOUS THROUGHOUT THE WORLD FOR FINE VEHICLES

"REGIS" SALOON

OIL-ENGINED DOUBLE-DECK BUS WITH STREAMLINE BODY

ELECTRIC TROLLEY-BUS

CROSSLEY MOTORS LTD. *Manchester and 50, Page Street, London, S.W.1.*

Obviously proud of its extended range of passenger vehicles, Crossley depicted a new trolleybus on the front of its publicity material. Coloured in the livery of Ashton, and carrying the fleet number 58, the artist's licence has contrived to produce a vehicle that certainly wasn't the No. 58 shown on page18! *(GLC)*

A Major Development

As has been mentioned previously, in 1908 a delegation from Manchester visited Germany to inspect a number of trolleybus installations. As a result, a decision in principle was taken to introduce 'trackless cars' where traffic levels did not support a tramway, although in the event, little else was done. In 1929 the innovative R Stuart Pilcher was appointed as General Manager with the Manchester Corporation Tramways Department, having previously been with the Edinburgh undertaking. Despite his considerable experience with trams, which was to see him introduce perhaps the most distinctive of cars to enter service in Manchester, and which in due course became referred to with his name, he nevertheless fully recognised the role the motorbus could play. On 6th April 1930, the Cheetham Hill to Stretford Road tramway was converted to motorbus operation, using the recently introduced lowbridge Leyland Titan model. This was one of the first major tram-to-motorbus conversions in the country, and from a financial point of view was an outstanding success. As a result, subsequent tramway abandonment for the next few years saw motorbuses being used as the replacements. In April 1935, however, elected members of Manchester City Council raised the question of the introduction of the trolleybus as a tram replacement, having regard to the fact that such a change would have economic benefits for the country, particularly as regards the use of home produced coal and a continuing load for the Corporation's electricity generating station. One also suspects that it had not escaped the attention of certain Councillors that other major cities, such as London, not to mention Birmingham, Bradford and Nottingham, were already operating trolleybuses.

Neither the General Manager, nor his Transport Committee, saw any benefit in changing what they viewed as their well established conversion policy, but the City Council thought otherwise. In July 1935, determined to seek detailed powers to operate trolleybuses, it postponed the transport department's plans to replace the Ashton Old Road trams with motorbuses. The result was that the successful promotion of a Parliamentary Bill led to the Manchester Corporation Act in April 1936.

The whole question of the motorbus versus trolleybus debate as suitable tramway replacement was not just a local one, and it is perhaps appropriate to pause for a moment to consider what was happening in the wider context. It was not simply a matter of which type of vehicle was cheaper to buy, but more a question of the relative operating expenses, and as far as the cost of electricity was concerned, this was a far from straightforward matter, as demonstrated by the reports in the trade journals.

In summary, the argument was, as in most cases, one of cost. And even then, the question of cost was clouded by the issue of what was

As explained in the text, the original Ashton route was an ideal testing ground for manufacturers to try out their products, and in Ashton Corporation they found a very willing and co-operative partner. Crossley built its first four-wheel trolleybus chassis in 1936, and since the line was only a matter of a few miles from their factory at Gorton, what could be more sensible than for it to be tested there. The rather strange appearance of the vehicle was necessitated by the need for a 'conning tower' type construction to carry the overhead collection gear. *(GLC)*

the true cost, and who should bear it. A representative of Salford Corporation was adamant that since both departments were in common ownership, the Transport section was not going to subsidise the Electricity section. Hull Council claimed they were in favour of trolleybuses because they were able to purchase electricity at cost. There was a general feeling that when a Council's Transport Department was the principal electricity user, it was not getting a fair price by comparison of what was charged to other industrial users. As general demand increased, the transport departments were not getting the benefits of a reduced price as a result of the extra demand. The debate was finely balanced and country-wide; Mr Ben England, at the time General Manager at Leicester, having produced a comprehensive report, recommended motorbuses as tramway

It was only to be expected that once Crossley had bodied the chassis it had trialled in Ashton, it would be returned to the facility where it had been tested. Although only eleven years separated the building of the two vehicles seen here, their appearance seems a generation apart! (STA)

replacements. On the other hand, Major McCreary, the Belfast General Manager, opted for trolleybuses, albeit initially as an experimental service on Falls Road. An editorial in *Bus & Coach* perhaps best summarised the situation; it urged that "the choice of vehicle should be made on the merits of each case. Too often a trolleybus undertaking finds itself burdened with an excessive charge for its traction current, and the result is liable to bring into disfavour a type of vehicle which, in other circumstances, has much to commend it".

Having to make plans, therefore, to introduce trolleybuses, the Manchester Committee made one further challenge to the full Council on the basis that the 43 vehicles required for the conversion were more expensive than their motorbus counterparts. Not surprisingly, their challenge was defeated, but the Council did permit the purchase of land at Rochdale Road for a new trolleybus garage, having initially preferred a site at Newton Heath.

Faced with such determination by the Council, the Transport Committee at last looked at the realism of the situation, and pointed out that just to convert the Ashton Old Road tram service was not really sensible in isolation, and that the Ashton

Crossley's first trolleybus had been put on show at Olympia in London in November 1935, and the following year it entered service on extended trial with Ashton Corporation. It was given the fleet number 58, following on from the original single-deck fleet. In this picture it has yet to registered. *(GLC)*

Ashton took delivery of additional trolleybuses in 1937 when three English Electric bodied Leyland TB5 models entered the fleet. They were rather confusingly numbered 48, 52 and 55 (the latter two numbers having become vacant on the withdrawal of the relevant single-deckers), and the combination of chassis and body manufacturer was subsequently to be repeated by Manchester in 1940. *(GLC)*

The first Crossley demonstrator seen on page 17 subsequently became Ashton No. 49 in 1937 and is seen here in the centre of Manchester outside what would later become the PTE's headquarters in this post-war view. (JC)

New Road services should also be included, as a result of which the order for new vehicles was eventually increased to 76.

Ashton, meanwhile, had been watching developments with interest. In any event it seemed inevitable that whatever future policy was decided, any major decision emanating from Manchester would see the end of Ashton's trams. It was first affected by Pilcher's motorbus-preferred approach when the Denton tram route succumbed in October 1936; six Crossley Mancunian motorbuses were the replacement on the joint service with Manchester. But whichever way the final decision in Manchester went, Ashton was not going to be left behind.

Crossley Motors of Gorton, whose works were situated between the two towns, was already a supplier to both the municipalities and was closely watching progress, not only in the North West, but across the municipal scene generally. The widespread interest in the trolleybus had not escaped them and they announced the availability of a new six-wheeled model for the November 1935 Commercial Motor Show, constructing a body with Metro-Cammell patented all-metal framing built in Birmingham, a feature that was to apply to all Crossley trolleybus bodies until after the war. This particular vehicle had echoes of London in its design, rather than the distinctive appearance that was to follow. It was registered CNE 74 and entered service on demonstration duties in May 1936, being painted in Ashton's livery of red, white and blue.

Ashton's small trolleybus operation was, at the time, the nearest to Crossley's works. Prior to the arrival of the demonstrator, a strange looking vehicle had already appeared on the Oldham Road service, again on demonstration, but initially not capable of carrying passengers. This was Crossley's first four-wheel trolleybus chassis on test, with a rudimentary open driving position, behind which was a small tower to which were fitted two trolley booms. It was subsequently fitted with a Metro-Cammell framed body by Crossley, almost identical to the bodies that were shortly to be supplied to Manchester. This time, the trolleybus was painted in Crossley's green and cream demonstration livery and the completed vehicle first appeared early in 1937. It was subsequently registered CTD 787 and became No. 49 in the Ashton fleet at the end of that year. The other demonstrator was also eventually taken into the Ashton fleet in June 1938, when it received

fleet number 58. In the meantime, Manchester's intentions having been confirmed, Ashton ordered a trio of trolleybuses from Leyland, which were fitted with English Electric bodies. Delivered in November 1937 and registered consecutively CTD 547 to 549, they were rather confusingly numbered 48, 52 and 55 in the fleet, the latter two numbers having initially been carried by the original single-deckers. At this time the pioneer Oldham Road trolleybus service between Ashton and Hathershaw must have presented a fine sight, as the remains of the 1925 Railless fleet operated alongside the more modern vehicles, both four-wheel and six-wheel, and from both Crossley and Leyland. Further variety was provided when Manchester's first trolleybus was tested over the same section.

It is interesting to note that this use of the Ashton - Hathershaw line for prototype testing was not confined to the late 1930s. It was also used for demonstration purposes by Ransomes, Sims and Jefferies in March 1927 (the vehicle ultimately going to St Helens), with a Preston-built English Electric single-decker being tested more than once between 1928 and 1930. Further visits from 'foreign' vehicles were made subsequently, although detailed records of their appearances have not survived. Mr Baker, writing in March 1931, commented that he had experimented very successfully with a double-deck trolleybus with pneumatic tyres on the service. The exact identity of this vehicle is not certain, although at this date candidates are limited. It may possibly have been one of AEC's original six-wheel chassis, and which was used extensively in connection with the introduction of trolleybuses in London. It has to be remembered that Ashton's pioneer route was by far the largest installation in the North West at the time when it opened, and was, therefore, the obvious location to use. Once the South Lancashire system, based in Atherton, was available, Leyland, amongst others, opted to use this facility for trolleybus testing.

Manchester's first trolleybus, No. 1000, is inspected by officials when obviously very new, not yet having been fitted with destination blinds. This was the first trolleybus to carry the standard Manchester streamline livery which was not to everyone's liking. Mr EC Ottaway, a technical officer with London Transport, when speaking at a meeting in Manchester early in 1938, observed that this style was only suited to an atmosphere of fun fairs and spectacular illuminations. (GLC)

Manchester Decides

While Ashton had been busily preparing itself for the withdrawal of its last trams, over in Manchester the Transport Committee, having reluctantly accepted that further opposition to the introduction of trolleybuses was fruitless, began making plans for the new network. It seems from the quality of the infrastructure that was ultimately provided, the General Manager was probably of the view that if the Council was insisting on the introduction of trolleybuses, then Manchester would have a system that was second to none. The tram services affected, which had received an extended life, but which were now to be converted, were 28 (Ashton & Piccadilly); 29 (Guide Bridge & Trafford Park) and 31 (Fairfield & Chorlton), all of which operated along Ashton Old Road. It was soon apparent, however, that to do this in isolation would have a detrimental effect on the common section of the Ashton New Road services between the Snipe Inn and Ashton, it not being sensible to have this section operated by both trolleybuses and trams. Accordingly, tram services 26 (Ashton & Stevenson Square) and 27 (Snipe & Stevenson Square) were incorporated into the scheme, with the result that 76 trolleybuses were now required, as mentioned previously.

Former tram services 29 and 31 were to be split into two sections, the southern sections to be operated by motorbuses, as it was not thought desirable to have both trolleybuses and trams operating together in the city centre, particularly in Market Street. This decision probably made sense at the time, but it ensured that the trolleybuses would never penetrate the important shopping area. As work commenced on the infrastructure required to permit the changeover, tenders were invited initially for 46 trolleybuses, equally split between the four- and six-wheel variety. A number of manufacturers submitted tenders, as follows:-

Company	4-wheel	6-wheel
Brush Electrical Co	£995	£1090
Cowieson & Co	£1500	£1600
Cravens	£960	£1037
Crossley	£995	£1090
English Electric	£995	£1090
Leyland Motors	no tender	£1035
MCW	£995	£1090
Park Royal	£995	£1090
Roe	£995	£1090
Strachans	£1092	£1152

The receipt of the brand new trolleybuses caused a series of official photographs to be taken, including the one above, and 1006, one of the Crossleys seen opposite, was the chosen vehicle for several posed views. The fleet name is shown in decorative style, but within a year or so it was changed to a simpler block style. Immediately below the first window behind the cab may be seen the holder for the running plate, a similar holder being fitted on the off-side. This system of running numbers, used on both motorbuses and trolleybuses, ceased just after the Second World War. *(GMTS both)*

Over the years unanswered questions have been asked about the Transport Committee's view of the existence of an apparent price ring. The writer takes the view that since over half of the organisations submitting tenders were only bodybuilders, and would have had to sub-contract the chassis construction anyway, it is not too strange to recognise that contact between the various suppliers must have taken place.

In the event, the order was actually placed, as mentioned, for 76 trolleybuses, as a result of the decision to include the Ashton New Road services. It was still equally split between four-wheelers and six-wheelers, and also almost equally between

Leyland and Crossley. The former were to supply 10 four-wheelers and 26 six-wheelers, the latter were to provide 28 four-wheelers and 12 six-wheelers. One might ask why Leyland was not favoured with all the six-wheelers, or what price was paid them for the four-wheelers, or why Cravens got nothing. One suspects the desire to support local industry was more a factor than purely price. Crossley's four-wheel trolleybus was, to all intents and purposes, a modified version of its 'Mancunian' motorbus chassis, although the weight of all the electrical equipment resulted in a vehicle weight in excess of the contemporary motorbus. The whole of the body contract went to Crossley, which was to build a trolleybus version of its then current motorbus body and, as previously mentioned, with Metro-Cammell patented all-metal frames. Fleet numbers were allocated as follows:-

1000 – 1027 Crossley four-wheel
1028 – 1037 Leyland four-wheel
1050 – 1061 Crossley six-wheel
1062 – 1087 Leyland six-wheel

The livery of the vehicles was similar to that introduced by the Corporation in 1936 in the

Robert Stuart Pilcher
General Manager, Manchester
1929-1946

A compulsory tilt test was required to be carried out on an example from each of the batches of new trolleybuses. Here No. 1051, one of the Crossley six-wheel models, completes the formalities. The vehicle would have been ballasted to replicate a typical passenger load, and once the test had been completed successfully, it was customary for a photograph of the test, with representatives of the manufacturer and operator present, to be taken. *(GMTS both)*

The brand new garage at Rochdale Road in Manchester was an impressive addition to the Transport Department's facilities. Throughout the expansion of trolleybus services during the 1930s, very few other operators provided amenities on a new site exclusively for the garaging of trolleybuses, it being more usually the case that the erstwhile tram depot was converted for use.

The overhead gantries suggest a total of six roads were available in the wide, uninterrupted expanse of the garage, which is well shown in this official view. Stacking of vehicles is arranged on the right hand side, with maintenance pits down the left. A closer view of the latter is shown on page 50. *(GMTS both)*

streamlined style of red and cream, as seen in the illustrations. For administrative purposes Manchester Corporation had, since 1933, allocated each batch of vehicles a class number. By the time the trolleybuses arrived, this series had reached 29, with the trolleybuses placed in a series starting at 90. The four batches above were given class numbers 90, 92, 91 and 93 respectively.

While the vehicles themselves were in build, work commenced on the construction of a new garage at Rochdale Road to accommodate them, which was to have a capacity of 115 vehicles. The building, as a brand new facility, gathered much coverage in the trade press. It could accommodate 100 trolleybuses in the covered parking area which measured 4,500 sq ft, while eight vehicles could be accommodated in the washing and inspection bay and seven in the repair bay. The building included a two-storey office block with dining room, kitchen and social room and a transformer house. The repair bay comprised six pits able to service 30 ft long vehicles and there was a Bendix-Cowdray brake testing plant at the entrance to the repair bay. A picture of this appears on page 50. Such features were not common in all transport undertakings, road runs utilising the good old Tapley meter being a cheaper but less efficient alternative. Perhaps once again Mr Pilcher had decided that if Manchester was to have trolleybuses, only the best facilities would suffice. Having said that, Huddersfield provided brake testing facilities in its Longroyd Bridge premises, which was under construction around the same time.

The alteration of the tramway overhead was a major task, so this work also began. Wherever possible, the standards used for the suspension of the tramway overhead were utilised for the trolleybus equipment. However, since both positive and negative lines had to be provided for the latter (the tram's electrical return was made through the track), additional or even replacement poles were frequently required. In some parts of the country contractors were employed for the overhead work, but in Manchester the Corporation carried out the work themselves. Ashton, on the other hand, hired an additional tower wagon from South Lancashire

One of the 12 Crossley pre-war 6-wheelers, No. 1055, at the exit to Rochdale Road garage, with the first of the class, No. 1050, hiding in the background. (*GMTS*)

This photograph in Ashton Old Road with No. 1064 was used extensively by Leyland in its pre-war publicity and was taken after the vehicle had presumably used the Fairfield Road turnback, despite the location of the poles on the overhead which would suggest otherwise! *(GLC)*

All-Crossley No. 1018 enters Piccadilly in this pre-war view about to take up service on the 29X short working along Ashton Old Road to Fairfield Road. The buildings in the background, on the corner of Portland Street and Parker Street, were destroyed in the 1940 blitz. *(RGRC)*

Ashton purchased a pair of Crossley 6-wheel trolleybuses in time for the start of services in March 1938. Again this is a post-war view. *(STA)*

Services Begin

On Tuesday 1st March 1938 the Lord Mayor of Manchester, Alderman JC Grime, formally opened Rochdale Road Garage and trolleybus operation in Manchester finally commenced. The same day saw the last tram running in Ashton - which ironically was a Manchester one! Before proceeding to the official luncheon which always seemed to accompany such events, various speeches were made and in the trade press reports that followed, the earlier confrontation over the whole question of the introduction of the trolleybuses was somewhat glossed over. However, Mr Pilcher took the opportunity to remind everyone that at a price of 0.73d a unit, electricity costs were too high. Generally the transport industry felt that the economic figure should not exceed 0.5d per unit.

The cost of electricity for traction purposes was one which was continuing to be contentious throughout the transport industry. In many cases the problem stemmed from the fact that the electricity department was a self-standing undertaking within the municipal structure. As tramcar services were converted to motor bus operation the amount of electricity being sold was dramatically reduced, causing problems for the profitability of the departments in question.

Nearby Salford typified the argument; the electricity department were taken with the prospect of having trolleybuses in the town, seeing an opportunity to retain the market for traction electricity. The Chairman of the Transport Committee was having none of it, however, stating publicly that he had no intention of propping up the ailing electricity department's finances.

Ben England, Leicester's General Manager, had stressed this in a report to his City Council, and Pilcher himself had, as President of the MTTA, been to France in 1930 to investigate the savings which could be made by using regenerative braking. His enthusiasm for this led to the MTTA purchasing equipment to be installed in one his tramcars, and, although that line of action was not implemented beyond the trials, when he was faced with having to have trolleybuses Pilcher quickly determined that he would seize that opportunity to reduce the Department's costs.

The new service carried the number 28, as had the trams it replaced, but it was extended to Stalybridge into the territory of Stalybridge, Hyde, Mossley and Dukinfield Tramways and Electricity Board's area. Trams between Stalybridge and Ashton had previously been operated jointly by the two undertakings. The SHMD Board was responsible for the overhead in its area, and had it not been for the outbreak of war, would almost certainly have become a further trolleybus operator in the North West. In Manchester City Centre the service terminated at Piccadilly. Vehicles from Ashton ran in via Fairfield Street and Aytoun Street to Portland Street, and left via Piccadilly and London Road. For emergency purposes a link was put in along Whitworth Street, subsequently being used by duplicate vehicles.

On the same day as the Ashton Old Road trolleybuses started, the Ashton New Road trams numbered 26 were withdrawn, the section between Audenshaw and Stevenson Square being strengthened by increased journeys on tram 26B. Additional trolleybuses on the converted 28 ensured there was no reduction in facilities over the Ashton section. Tramcar services along Ashton Old Road on the 31 finally ceased when trolleybus service 29 was introduced between Audenshaw (The Trough) and Piccadilly from 21st March 1938. Eventually, sufficient new trolleybuses of the Manchester order for 76 having been delivered, tramcar operation along Ashton New Road finally ceased on 30th July 1938, and on the following day new trolleybus services 26 (Ashton & Stevenson Square) and 27 (Audenshaw (The Snipe) & Stevenson Square) commenced, both operated exclusively by Manchester Corporation. The terminal arrangements at The Snipe were unusual in that to turn, trolleybuses had to reverse into Gainsborough Road, the only location where this happened. As a matter of interest, The Snipe was the boundary point between Manchester and Ashton. Geoff Hyde records that under pressure from Ashton, Manchester were persuaded, in February 1939, to extend the 26 trolleybus service from Ashton to Stalybridge. The same month saw the abandonment of the original trolleybus service

between Ashton and Hathershaw, the original vehicles and equipment being life-expired, and Ashton having been unable to persuade the latter to reintroduce electric vehicles between the two towns. The replacement motorbus service was, in fact, operated through to Rochdale, being operated jointly by the three municipalities.

Further Plans

Towards the end of 1938 Manchester's General Manager had prepared a report on further tramway conversions. Conversion to trolleybus was still only considered as 'possible', but the list was as follows:-

Tram 51	Miller Street & University via Ardwick
Tram 19	Victoria Street & Hyde
Tram 33	Victoria Street & Reddish via Belle Vue
Tram 34A	Piccadilly & Belle Vue
Bus 15	Piccadilly & Guide Bridge
Bus 57	Ashton & Haughton Green via Denton

The 57 service was jointly operated with Ashton Corporation. Certain of the above proposals lent themselves to conversion, insofar as trolleybus overhead already existed over some of the proposed new service. For example, as far as the 51 tram was concerned, from Rochdale Road around to Ashton Old Road it was in place for the services already introduced and their associated depot workings. The Haughton Green route was already covered as far as Guide Bridge. The proposals received the approval of the City Council in February 1939 and as a first step, tenders were invited for an additional 77 trolleybuses to operate the services that the proposals encompassed. Extracts from this tender, which was issued on 25th February 1939, show that among items listed for each vehicle under the 'Sundry Fittings' heading in the tender were 15 Match Strikers, three Guard's loading mirrors (Conductors in Manchester were always described as 'Guards'), which were fitted so that upper saloon and gangway were visible from the platform; the platform and step were visible from the upper saloon, the third mirror being fitted to the arch panel on the rear bulkhead, two Driver's mirrors (all the mirrors were to be acid etched 'M.C.T.D.' – to deter bathroom improvers?), one pair of rubber gloves (this was a Ministry of Transport requirement rather than purely a Manchester one),

Ashton's first war-time deliveries were eight Crossley trolleybuses, virtually to the design of Manchester's 1001-27, registered ETE 811-8. Number 57 is seen above towards the end of its life in Ashton Market Place. *(STA)*

A rear view of one of the same batch shows that Ashton only fitted one number plate at the back, illumination at night being by the lighting from the lower saloon. The photograph dates from 1951. *(IY)*

and one Bamboo Pole Trolley Retriever. The whole document was produced in a manner that one would expect from an organisation the size of Manchester Corporation's Transport Department; one suspects that similar documents produced by Ashton might not have been quite as comprehensive!

Work on the next extension to the overhead then commenced at Audenshaw, where a spur off the 28 service from The Trough ran along Audenshaw Road to Guide Bridge. This was opened as the 29 service from 16th October 1939, vehicles on the old 29 service between The Trough and City becoming numbered 31.

War Intervenes

We have already seen that despite the outbreak of war, Manchester had continued to implement its proposals agreed in early 1939. The 29 trolleybus service had reached Guide Bridge by October, although the day war was declared, 3rd September 1939, had, at one stage, been the date it had been intended to introduce the Hyde Road conversion. By that date work had begun on the replacement of worn or inadequate tramway poles, but no overhead had yet been erected. Nevertheless, work was continuing on the conversion of two other services, to the extent that the Guide Bridge overhead had been extended along Stockport Road to Chester Square, this section being within Ashton Corporation's area, who completed the work, allowing service 29 to continue into Ashton under the existing facilities, with the result that from 22nd March 1940 service 29 became jointly operated by both Ashton and Manchester trolleybuses. The other service where work was taking place was the one to Manchester University. The tram service, which was numbered 51, was replaced by a temporary motorbus service on 24th March 1940, so that work could be completed in daylight hours in order to introduce the trolleybuses from 6th April 1940. Over the years, much of the work on trolleybus overhead was carried out at night to avoid disrupting the service; under the blackout circumstances pertaining at the time this was obviously not possible.

The new trolleybus service was numbered 30, and operated between Rochdale Road and the University. For some of its length the route was able to use existing overhead; this included the 'inner' terminal which utilised Swan Street (interestingly, it was in the offices of the Baker's Institute in Swan Street that the inaugural meeting of the Tramway Museum Society was held), Rochdale Road, Thompson Street and Oldham Road overhead which was in situ for access to the Rochdale Road Garage. The service then ran along Great Ancoats Street, jointly with the Ashton New Road services, before crossing the Ashton Old Road services at Pin Mill Brow. Through Ardwick the service was breaking new ground, although the Hyde service was eventually to cross it, much later than originally planned, at Ardwick Green. The service then reached the University via Brunswick Street, turning via New York Street, Eldon Street and Rumford Street back onto Brunswick Street. The 30 was a somewhat strange service, never really penetrating any of the city area, but running in a crescent shape around the east of the city centre, and eventually crossing all of the other trolleybus services which ran along five orbital roads.

In common with vehicles throughout the country, certain protective measures were taken soon after the outbreak of war. The principal concern was the level of lighting after dark, which it was felt might assist enemy aircraft in their bombing raids. All streets lights were switched off and on the vehicles both interior and exterior lighting was reduced, with white paint being applied to the edges of buses to assist with recognition in the blackout. The light coloured roofs were painted grey. The driving of any vehicle at night was, therefore, extremely taxing.

In light of the proposals in the 1938 report outlined above, Ashton had, in fact, ordered a further eight vehicles from Crossley (these were registered ETE 811-18, and took the vacant fleet numbers between 50 and 60), and were almost identical to Manchester's 1000 - 1027 batch, Ashton's vehicles being available for the extended 29 service. Over in Manchester, the first of the City's second order for 77 trolleybuses were arriving, and fleet numbers were allocated as follows:-

1100 - 1136 Leyland four-wheel; 1137 - 1176 Crossley four-wheel. They were included in class numbers 92 and 90 respectively. The Crossley vehicles had bodies almost identical to the original batch, although the seating was improved, having higher backs, in line with Manchester's then standard specification. The Leyland trolleybuses, on the other hand, were a radical departure from previous deliveries, in that the bodies were built by English Electric in Preston, although they were designed to resemble the standard Manchester streamlined body. The keen-eyed could, nevertheless, detect detailed differences. Manchester obviously thought they were similar enough to categorise them in the same class as the pre-war Leylands. Whereas the manufacture of both buses and trolleybuses was initially suspended by the National Government on the outbreak of war, as all the materials were in hand for these new trolleybuses delivery continued right into 1943.

In July 1940 a further joint Ashton/Manchester trolleybus service was opened, numbered 57, running from Ashton Market Place to Denton. This replaced motorbuses which had in turn replaced the 57 tram in 1936. A considerable section of this route was already in use by the 29 trolleybus between Ashton and Guide Bridge, but from here the route branched south to its terminus, which was only temporary. In December 1940 it was further extended from Denton to Haughton Green,

in line with the 1938 proposals. The actual opening of this section may well have been affected by the worsening emergency. This was an interesting service as far as Manchester was concerned, for any vehicle working on the 57 was a long way from its own depot in Manchester. It was probably just as well that from the start of joint trolleybus operation reciprocal arrangements existed between the two undertakings whereby a defective trolleybus away from its home town could, and would, be replaced by a vehicle from the joint operator's fleet.

The 57 was, in fact, worked from Hyde Road; the garage part of the depot had already been in use for trolleybuses following the introduction of the 30 service.

Orders for the next stage of the trolleybus scheme in Manchester were again split between Crossley and Leyland, but this time the latter vehicles received bodies by English Electric built in Preston. Number 1136, seen here before delivery, carries the revised style of fleet name and grey roof. *(STA)*

By now the impact of the war was beginning to be felt quite severely, air raids on Manchester and the North West becoming common place. The City Council, in the light of the worsening situation, announced in September 1940, that for the time being, it was not to proceed with the conversion of the Hyde Road service, for which 44 trolleybuses had been earmarked and were in the course of delivery. Instead, the vehicles would be used to replace motorbuses on service elsewhere and thus save fuel oil, a major reason for the change of plans.

Below we see a fine if misty rear view of No. 1107, one of the thirty-seven 1940 Crossleys, with the Transport Department's offices at 55 Piccadilly, in the background. Note the 'O' for 'overhead' placed strategically on the rear off-side corner, to remind other trolleybus drivers not to overtake. *(GMTS)*

Moston Chosen

The motorbus services concerned served Moston, New Moston, Collyhurst, Harpurhey and Blackley. There were a number of reasons for this decision. The Moston area services ran right outside Rochdale Road Garage and, therefore, no additional wiring for depot journeys would be required. When the tram services along Rochdale Road had been replaced by motorbuses, a fair number of traction poles had remained for street lighting purposes, thus reducing the requirement for new equipment, and finally it was found that the electricity supply to the area was robust enough to accommodate the extra demand trolleybuses required. It was not possible under the circumstances to order new equipment, so that intended for the Hyde Road conversion would have to do. Neither was it possible to obtain the necessary Parliamentary powers to authorise the operation of this group of routes, and so it was eventually agreed between the Government and the Council that, provided the Council obtained the requisite powers when it was able to do so, work on the conversion could proceed.

This work erecting the new trolleybus overhead began in June 1940, and when it reached the Rochdale Road/Moston Lane junction, a connection was provided for the intended service to Blackley Estate. This destination was furthermore incorporated on the destination blinds of the 1100-class buses then in the course of delivery. But once more the plans of the Transport Department were thwarted, when it was established that the electrical supply to the estate was actually not robust enough to accommodate a service of trolleybuses. Accordingly, the equipment intended for this area was used instead to extend the Moston service to the Ben Brierley Hotel, to convert the Oldham Road to Moston service, and to subsequently extend both services to the Gardener's Arms in New Moston.

The first of these facilities was introduced from 4th November that year when the 55 motorbus was replaced by a trolleybus service carrying the same number. It ran from Stevenson Square, already served by the 26 and 27 trolleybuses, via Rochdale Road to Moston. In Moston, the service ran clockwise via Rochdale Road, Moston Lane, Upper Conran Street and Conran Street in the mornings, and in the afternoons anti-clockwise. During the winter of 1940/1 the city was badly blitzed, but generally the trolleybus network was unaffected, being a little way from the principal targets, namely the docks and the railway stations. The introduction of new services during this time could not have been easy, however, as even an air raid warning that might subsequently turn out to be a false alarm would have disrupted work. Nevertheless, as seen on page 37, No. 1081 did suffer damage as the result of an air raid in August 1940. The nights of 22nd and 23rd December were particularly severe in terms of air raids, and some re-instatement was necessary in the Rochdale Road area. This area was not that far from Victoria Station and the railway yard at Red Bank, an obvious target for enemy bombers. It may well be that raids such as these had some detrimental effect on the work of introducing new services. Certainly many fine buildings in the city centre were destroyed by the December raids.

By early 1941 it was, nevertheless, found possible to extend the Moston service to Ben Brierley; the opportunity being taken at that stage to renumber it to 32, short workings to Moston Lane showing 60X or 32X. This fairly regular renumbering of services was to become a feature of the Moston operation. The city terminal working was altered in June 1941 to operate inwards via Shude Hill and High Street, terminating in Church Street and departing along Oldham Street and Oldham Road as before. Wiring was opened to Nuthurst Road from 14th July 1941; on that date the 37 trolleybus service was introduced from Stevenson Square along Oldham Road replacing the northern half of the 80 motorbus service. From the same date the 32 was also extended to Nuthurst Road.

By now Rochdale Road Garage had received its full complement of trolleybuses, and from the date of the Nuthurst Road extension, contemporary reports indicate that Hyde Road Depot was opened to trolleybuses. However, the number of trolleybuses delivered before this date was more than Rochdale Road could accommodate and Hyde Road was already in use as indicated previously, probably from March 1940. From July 1941 Hyde Road took over the working of the 28 and 29 services, which geographically were the closest to it. Thus commenced a relationship between the trolleybus services in Piccadilly and Hyde Road Depot which was to continue until the last day of trolleybus operation. Finally, on 2nd August 1941 the Nuthurst Road services were extended to the Gardener's Arms. Yet again a recasting of the

Reference is made in the text to the damage sustained by Leyland TTB4 No. 1081 on August 1940. Wartime photography was severely restricted, generally on the grounds of security, but these official views clearly show the damage sustained in what was described as a 'bomb explosion'. *(GMTS)*

Two contrasting views taken from the MCTD offices at 55 Piccadilly, which overlooked the trolleybus terminus of the Ashton Old Road services. In between the photographs being taken, the buildings at the top of Portland Street have disappeared as a result of the blitz. The area to the right, occupied by wartime air raid shelters, has recently seen the construction of new offices. *(GMTS)*

service numbers was introduced. Oldham Road 'shorts' to Ben Brierley retained 37, but the extended service was 36. The main Rochdale Road service retained 32, but the Ben Brierley service became 33. Journeys to Moston Lane/Conran Street became 33X. Nuthurst Road 'shorts' were 32X or 36X as appropriate.

The country was now going through the darkest days of the war, and it is perhaps not surprising that there is little to record in terms of changes for almost the next two years; it is also possible, of course, that during this time records were not maintained to peacetime standards for a variety of reasons. The next change was, in fact, directly related to the war effort. AV Roe had established a factory at Greengate for aircraft production and a private bus station had been provided adjacent to the works. The services terminating at Gardener's Arms were, therefore, extended in June 1943 at peak times for approximately half a mile along Greengate to the factory, which was actually in Chadderton, some several hundred yards beyond the city boundary. A few weeks after this extension was provided, delivery of the last of the 77 trolleybuses ordered in 1939 (No. 1175) arrived, still to peace-time standards. It has, in fact, been beyond the writer's knowledge to identify any other large batch of vehicles, constructed to peacetime standards, delivered so far into the wartime period.

Manchester's trolleybus fleet at that stage stood at an impressive total of 153 units, all less than six years old, and well able to deal with the heavy demands placed upon it initially by wartime conditions. Ashton, on the other hand, was not quite so well placed to meet these heavier and unforeseen levels of increased traffic demand, and needed to take steps to rectify this situation. Under the emergency regulations drawn up jointly by the Ministry of Supply and the Ministry of War Transport, a scheme for the construction and delivery of wartime buses was developed. As with all manufacture at the time, a somewhat restricted specification was drawn up, and this came to be known as the 'utility' specification. This was applied to both buses and trolleybuses, and limited numbers of both chassis and body-builders were selected to produce these products. As far as the trolleybus industry was concerned, only one chassis was involved, built at Sunbeam Commercial Vehicles in Wolverhampton, who produced its W4 (wartime, four-wheel) model. A total of 468 were constructed, slightly less than half of which carried Karrier badges, as a result of the takeover of Karrier Motors Ltd by the Rootes Group in 1935. Rootes was the parent company of Sunbeam from the same year.

Allocation of these wartime models was by the Ministry of War Transport, depending on the applicant for new vehicles meeting the Ministry's criteria for provision. The period of time between the request for new vehicles being submitted and delivery taking place could be quite lengthy, and it is not known exactly when Ashton's requisition was made. However, in October 1944 Nos. 61 and 62 entered service, being Sunbeam Ws with Park Royal 56-seat utility bodywork. A further pair, Nos. 63 and 64, of the same combination, were to enter service a month later. In keeping with the circumstances of the time, they were fitted with wooden slatted seats, which tended to give a somewhat uncomfortable ride over the sett-paved streets of the day! All were delivered in a rather drab overall grey livery, but as soon as peacetime conditions permitted, they were repainted into Ashton's extremely attractive red, white and blue scheme. This quartet was unique among all the trolleybuses delivered to Ashton and Manchester (other than the original ten vehicles) in that the electrical equipment was supplied by English Electric, rather than Metro-Vick.

The first true wartime trolleybus deliveries to either operator, that is, a vehicle built to emergency utility specification, arrived with Ashton in October 1944, when a pair of Park Royal bodied Sunbeam Ws were taken into stock. A further pair, of the same combination, entered service the following month. They were numbered 61-4, and registered FTE 645-8. *(RGRC)*

Two more utility trolleybuses, Nos. 65/6, were delivered in 1946, this time with Roe utility bodies. Neither Park Royal nor Roe had been suppliers to Ashton previously, but the latter was subsequently to become a regular supplier to the Corporation. *(GMTS)*

As a result of the war, standards of maintenance suffered considerably. In this post-war view, one of Ashton's 1940 Crossleys heads three Manchester vehicles in Piccadilly. *(STA)*

Peacetime Returns

As the War in Europe moved closer to its final stages, there was a gradual return to peacetime conditions. As the threat of air raids receded, the blackout restrictions were relaxed. From 25th April 1945, new regulations were introduced revising the previous constraints and operators moved quickly to restore lighting conditions to pre-war standards. In terms of new vehicles and new routes it was, however, to be a little while before the pre-war plans could be 'dusted off' and put into effect. Some of these earlier proposals were not to come to fruition; had the War not intervened the SHMD Board would undoubtedly have become the North West's next trolleybus operator; after the War this simply did not happen. The priority as far as the country and the government was concerned was to get back on its feet financially as soon as possible, which included much emphasis on exports, so for the time being austerity measures were likely to continue.

None of the above should suggest that the operators were 'taking a breather' after their Herculean efforts during the War; before the end of 1945 Manchester initiated work on the extension of the No. 30 trolleybus service from the University to Greenheys (Platt Lane). 1946 was to see this work continue and indeed the year was to be quite a busy one. Nevertheless, the die was cast as far as trolleybuses in Manchester were concerned when, early in the year, the Transport Department announced its intention to abandon the remaining

tramways as soon as possible, using trolleybuses for the Hyde route only, and motorbuses elsewhere. Progress on the No. 30 service saw it extended to Moss Lane East on 14th January and to Platt Lane with effect from the 20th February. The extension was particularly useful for dealing with football crowds, as it served Manchester City's ground at Maine Road, this famous address being close to Lloyd Street as used by the No. 30 trolleybus service. Deprived of so many sporting occasions during the War, the opening of the 1946/7 Football League season on 31st August 1946 saw crowds once again flocking to Maine Road for football matches. The service doubly benefited in this connection as rivals Manchester United were unable to use their Old Trafford ground until 1949, it having been badly bomb damaged during the war and, therefore, shared Maine Road with City. Trolleybuses were operated direct from Moston, Audenshaw and Edge Lane to Platt Lane on Match days, but regrettably photographic illustrations of this operation have once again proved, so far, elusive.

February 1946 also saw Ashton place two more utility Sunbeam trolleybuses into service, but this time the bodywork was supplied by Roe. The middle of the year was to see changes at the very top of the organisation, when R Stuart Pilcher's

An early decision of Manchester's new General Manager was to abandon the pre-war streamlined livery. In this photograph, the leading vehicle still retains its two 'swoops' but the following one has already had the upper one painted over. *(GMTS)*

tenure as Manchester's General Manager came to an end. He was succeeded by AF Neal, who was returning to the City's Transport Department from Edinburgh, after joining them in 1938, but as far as policy was concerned, it was to be very much as before, as this change of manager did not herald any startling changes in direction. Also on the administrative front, it was necessary for Manchester Corporation to 'legalise' the Moston operations, by obtaining the appropriate powers that the War had prevented. The result was the 1946 Act, wherein Part III legitimatised the wartime provisions. The Act also provided powers to operate along Manor Road in Droylsden, which was not to begin until agreement with A Mayne & Son had been reached. Such agreement, although eventually reached, was not to have implications for any new trolleybus services.

Early 1947 witnessed work commencing (or perhaps more accurately, 're-commencing') on the long awaited Hyde service, and by the end of the year most of the new overhead was in place, with the exception of certain junctions. It was to be a year or so yet, however, before trolleybuses were to appear on a service that was ideal for such vehicles, having many long, straight sections. During this period the original pre-war plans were modified, of which more shortly. In the meantime, the first of the post-war renumbering of services took place when the joint No. 57 from Ashton to Haughton Green became 17, thus placing it closer to the other trolleybus service numbers, although this was, perhaps, a strange choice, as this number

was already in use for the joint motorbus service between Manchester and Rochdale. Perhaps it was an indication that trams, trolleybuses and motorbuses were viewed separately at Piccadilly (Manchester's head office). As an example, at one time each type had its own service numbered 33!

New Vehicles

In order to operate this new service, it was obviously necessary to order new rolling stock. This time Crossley was selected to supply 54 complete vehicles. By now they had been taken over by the Associated Equipment Company Limited of Southall (AEC), the parent company becoming Associated Commercial Vehicles (ACV) soon after. Once again there was to be a mix of four- and six-wheel vehicles; this time there were to be 38 of the former (which were to become Fleet Nos. 1200-37 – class 94) and 16 of the latter (Fleet Nos. 1240-55 – class 95). The four-wheel model was given the designation 'Empire' by Crossley; the six-wheel version was called the 'Dominion'. One significant change from previous deliveries was the fact that these trolleybuses were 8ft wide, Manchester standardising on this dimension not long after this width became legal. Only two other operators were

The first post-war trolleybuses delivered to Manchester eventually arrived in 1949. Here the first, No. 1201, undergoes the compulsory tilt test which was normally recorded for confirmation that the tilt was satisfactorily accomplished, something the Certifying Officer needed to be able to verify. The livery has been changed, and a new style of fleet number has been introduced. *(GMTS)*

An official view of No. 1208 shows that the livery changes are still in the process of development, as a fleet name is not displayed, nor have destination blinds yet been fitted. *(GLC)*

supplied with Empire models; Manchester was unique in receiving the Dominion. This choice of such patriotic names for Crossley's Electric Passenger models seems a little quaint nearly sixty years later, when anything smacking of colonial influence is shunned; but in the aftermath of the War, when the role and contribution of Britain's Commonwealth cousins was widely recognised, such a gesture undoubtedly seemed perfectly normal.

It was, however, to be some time before this order was to be delivered, and the delay in arrival was to see the Hyde trams firstly replaced by buses before trolleybuses took over and, indeed, Manchester's last tram ran over a year before this was to happen. From Crossley's point of view, they had more than enough work producing motorbuses to permit resources to be diverted into the production of what were to be, after, only a minority type for them. As a reflection of the national situation mentioned above, in 1945 the Netherlands Railways placed an order for 1,175 Crossley chassis. This work kept Crossley busy for the next four years; Manchester Corporation itself ordered nearly 300 Crossley buses after the War. In any case the Ministry of Supply was still determining priorities - no wonder the building of the trolleybuses had to wait!

Final Years of the Decade

1948 saw further renumbering of trolleybus services. At this stage it is not clear whether the grouping of the trolleybus service numbers into the 200 series was envisaged; the renumbering that took place on 12th July 1948 did not seem to indicate that this was so! The 36 (Gardener's Arms) became the 31; the 37 (Ben Brierley) became the 31X; 36X (Nuthurst Road) was no longer used. The 31, 31X (Audenshaw or Fairfield Street) were renumbered back to 29X, thus re-using the number used by the trams. From the same day the 30 was extended to Corporation Street. Ever since this service had begun its terminal was short of any real traffic objective; for convenience sake it had used the loop around Swan Street, Rochdale Road, Thompson Street and Oldham Road. The extension took it along Miller Street and left into Corporation Street, returning via Redfern Street to Miller Street.

This brought the service closer to Victoria Station and the business area of the city. When operating from town, it was still necessary to negotiate three sides of the Thompson Street rectangle.

The end of tram services was now not far away, and this included the joint service to Stockport. It might have been thought that long straight sections, along Wellington Road for example, would have been ideal for trolleybuses, but perhaps with Stockport's it was a case of 'once bitten', so motorbuses were the replacement. January 10th 1949 saw the final Manchester tram complete its ceremonial last journey, while three months later the first of the new Crossley trolleybuses entered service. Ashton had also ordered five Empire models; the first of these was delivered in the final weeks of the year and were almost identical to the Manchester order, although whereas Manchester's post-war livery was much simplified, Ashton retained its red, white and blue scheme. The only other British trolleybus operator to receive Crossleys post-war was Cleethorpes, whose two Empire models (but with Roe bodywork) distinguished themselves when they became the only vehicles of their marque to work for two operators when they were sold to Walsall in 1960.

The livery applied to Manchester's new vehicles was all-over red, with cream around the upper-deck windows and a cream band above the lower-deck windows. One of the new General Manager's early decisions had been to phase out the streamlined livery, but this did not happen overnight, and partial repaints, which circumstances of the time dictated, meant that vehicles could be seen in various stages of the transformation. The roof was painted red to signify, as was the Corporation's practice at the time, that the vehicle was eight feet wide. In any event, light coloured roofs, certainly around the rear dome, were not practical, as dirty water, grease and carbon dripping from the overhead booms was partially hidden by this darker shade. Even the pre-war trolleybuses had their rear domes painted red (in lieu of cream) after the War. The bold 'Manchester Corporation' name, which had appeared on the rear of previous deliveries, was to disappear to be replaced by a panel for an advertisement, but a few were delivered with this feature. This time Crossley produced its own metal-framing for the body, so the vehicles truly were all-Crossley products, although by this time they were not actually built in Manchester, but at

Ashton once more took a batch of vehicles into stock which were similar to deliveries to Manchester. Number 77 is posed at Stamford Park prior to entering service. *(GMTS)*

Errwood Park. This location was situated not far from the city boundary at Levenshulme, actually in Heaton Chapel, Stockport and the site to which Crossley moved from Gorton in 1947.

Into the Fifties

At long last sufficient of the new trolleybuses had been delivered to permit their introduction on the Manchester to Hyde service, which occurred on 16th January 1950. The terminus of the 210 was in George Street at the other end of Piccadilly from the terminus of the 218 and 219 services. Originally it had been intended that there would be a short branch off Hyde Road along Reddish Lane to Reddish, but when this section became the focus of proposals for a cross city service (eventually becoming part of the joint Manchester/Salford 57/ 77 services between Swinton and Pendlebury and Reddish), it was never wired. Instead, the service was extended beyond Hyde town centre, the original

planned terminus, to Gee Cross. In preparation for the original proposals, as long back as 1939, the SHMD Board had provided overhead at Hyde Market Place along Newton Street, George Street and Clarendon Street; this was never connected to the through service but remained in place for some years. SHMD had, in fact, responsibility for the maintenance of the infrastructure from the city boundary at Broomstairs Bridge to Gee Cross, as well, of course, as the section from Stamford Park to Stalybridge. In view of the small number of trolleybuses that would have been required to operate SHMD's share of the service, the Board declined to obtain any trolleybuses, and permitted Manchester to cover its share. The service was the first operated by trolleybuses to use a route number in the 200 series, becoming 210, and replacing the 106 motorbus service, which in turn had replaced the trams from 14th March 1948. Initial post-war proposals had suggested that the route number 24 would have been used.

Shortly after the introduction of the 210, the next stage of the 'grouping' of trolleybus route numbers occurred when, on 17th April, the 215, 216, 217, 218 and 219 were introduced, formerly being 27, 26, 17, 28 and 29 respectively, all with matching changes to the 'X' number where used.

It was not until October 1951 that the last of the 54 new trolleybuses entered service, the four-

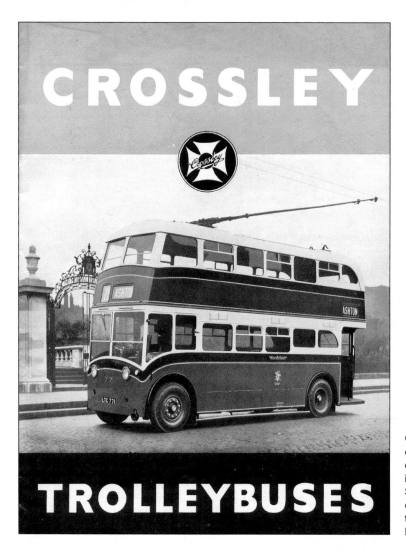

CROSSLEY

TROLLEYBUSES

Crossley utilised a view of one of the post-war Ashton deliveries, this time facing in the opposite direction at Stamford Park, to fill the cover of its brochure for the new Empire and Dominion chassis. *(GLC)*

wheel Empire models being joined by the first of the six-wheel Dominion type from March 1951. The final delivery of these vehicles was significant in that they represented the final Crossley-badged vehicles to enter the Manchester Corporation fleet. By this date, withdrawal of the very first of the pre-war trolleybuses had commenced, a handful of the six-wheel types going first. The next stage of the service renumbering was introduced on 21st April 1952, when the 30 became the 213.

The two types of post-war vehicle were to remain the mainstay of the 210 service for all of its life; when not required on the 210, the four-wheel examples might be found on the 213, 217, 218 or 219. The six-wheel specimens tended to lead a rather sheltered life, being mainly, but not exclusively, employed on part-day duties on the 210 and the 213X and 218X. The trolleybus

services were now at their maximum extent, with a total route length of 44 miles and it is, therefore, perhaps the time to break off from relating sequential details to examine some of the features necessary to support the operation of trolleybuses, and which makes their study so fascinating.

Behind the Scenes

When the trolleybus services were introduced into Manchester a decision was taken to keep the power supply to the trolleybus system separate from the trams. There may have been good reasons for doing this; one that springs to the writer's mind is that in so doing the operational management would have been easier, for a fault, for example, in an electrical sub-station might only disable one of the networks

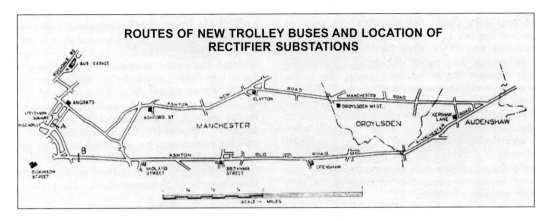

ROUTES OF NEW TROLLEY BUSES AND LOCATION OF
RECTIFIER SUBSTATIONS

Reproduced from *Passenger Transport* for March 1938, courtesy DS Hellewell

in an area, rather than both. It was also possibly the case that the true costs of operating trolleybuses could be more clearly identified. This arrangement meant, as an illustration, that where trolleybuses still shared roads with trams, unique overhead was provided for both sets of vehicle. Whilst this was not completely unusual in the country, it was perhaps more usual for trams to share the positive overhead line for their supply once trolleybus overhead was erected. It should be noted that the normal convention with trolleybus overhead wires was that the positive wire was that nearest the centre of the road, whilst the negative one was nearest to the pavement.

One distinct disadvantage of this arrangement was that where tram and trolleybus overhead crossed there was a long dead section, provided by an insulator, longer than would have been the case with the more usual arrangement. It also meant that trams and trolleybuses were more likely to come to a halt on dead sections, as a result of which they had either to be pushed across it by another tram, or moved on battery in the case of a trolleybus (all of Manchester's trolleybuses were fitted with battery equipment enabling them to move under their own power for a short distance). More seriously, however, was the fact that these longer dead sections frequently gave rise to blue flashes when they were crossed with power on. The correct driving procedure in the case of both trams and trolleybuses was to 'coast' (ie roll with no power being drawn) under dead sections, but the initial Manchester style made this more difficult.

The blue flashes were bad enough under normal circumstances, as the arcing and burning had a tendency over time to damage the overhead wires, but in wartime it was felt that such flashes would be visible to the Luftwaffe in hours of darkness. Pressure from both the Air Ministry and the Police led to this separate electrical supply system being abandoned, and Philip Groves observed during a visit to the city centre early in 1941 that revised arrangements had been introduced, so that the insulation between the trolleybus positive wire and the tramway wire had been removed.

Power in Manchester was initially supplied by the Corporation's Electricity Department, but following nationalisation in 1948, it was purchased from the North Western Electricity Board. At maximum, a total of 21 sub-stations, sited approximately a couple of miles or so apart, were provided in Manchester, where the ac supply was converted to dc for the overhead. These had a rectifier capacity of either 375 or 500kw. Four of the sub-stations were equipped with rotary converters, the others being of the alternative mercury arc type. At about one mile intervals, although closer in the city centre, the cables from the sub-stations were fed into section boxes on the street, and then up the traction standard to the overhead section. These sections were isolated from each other so that a fault in one section would not affect a whole route, although they could be linked if required.

The ability to link sections was greatly facilitated by a device known as a 'Hastings Coupler', which had been developed by the Hastings Tramways Company, a trolleybus operator on the South Coast. They had developed an automatic switching device which was installed in the section boxes associated with the section insulators normally separating the substations to enable them to be coupled together. They had done

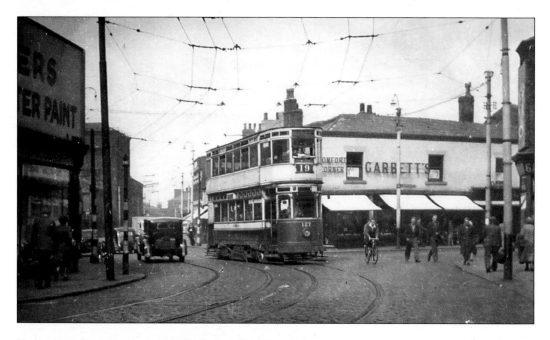

The system of keeping tram and trolleybus overhead separate, used extensively in the centre of Manchester, is clearly shown in this view, above, actually taken in the centre of Hyde. *(JSKC)*

In today's safety critical industrial climate, such a scene would be unthinkable. But if a tower wagon was not handy, the only way to inspect and repair trolley heads was to use the emergency door at the rear of the upper deck. Some operators specified a solid panel in the emergency exit in order to provide a safe working platform for the linesman or fitter. *(STA)*

BUT-built No. 1318 inches past one of the Guy Vixen overhead wagons at Audenshaw. The vehicle is within feet of an overhead skate which would set the points seen at the top of the picture. In this view it would seem that it is the overhead that required attention rather than the vehicle. *(STA)*

Ashton's choice for maintaining the trolleybus overhead for which it was responsible was the ubiquitous normal-control Bedford, an example of which is seen here in Ashton's bus station, a location which trolleybuses never succeeded in penetrating. *(STA)*

Reference has been made to the well appointed facilities provided in Rochdale Road Garage. Here brand new Crossley No. 1051 stands over one of the several pits provided for routine maintenance, whilst in the foreground the brake testing equipment supplied by Bendix-Cowdray can be seen. *(GMTS)*

At regular intervals of around one mile, section feeders could be seen. This particular installation is unusual in that because it is supplying the loop it is single feed, rather than a double one. The feeder box, which allowed sections to be isolated if necessary, is actually on the pavement approximately 100 yards from the feeder. *(JSK)*

Rochdale Road Garage was a brand new facility built for trolleybuses, whereas in the case of most (but not all) other tram-to-trolleybus conversions the premises previously used by the trams sufficed. The typical late-1930s brick structure, of strictly functional nature, was designed by Mr G Noel Hill, the Manchester City Architect, and was extremely well equipped, in line with Pilcher's determination that his city's trolleybus system should be the best that could be procured. Vertical folding doors were state of the art; see the earlier models below! *(JAS)*

The Mossley Road garage of Ashton Corporation, which housed their trolleybus fleet, was converted from the original premises constructed for trams. This resulted in the requirement for vehicles leaving the covered area to have to be reversed out onto the yard. *(RGR)*

Parked outside Mossley Road garage are Manchester No. 1315 and Ashton No. 54, an interesting comparison of post- and pre-war trolleybuses. The reciprocal arrangements between the two undertakings for breakdown cover meant that Manchester vehicles were no strangers to Ashton's garage. *(STA)*

this to reduce the load on their central area in order to avoid a punitive tariff at peak times. The Hastings Coupler was also a necessary tool on systems that utilized regenerative trolleybuses, as Manchester did. Substations were equipped with resistance load banks which were arranged to be switched in whenever excess power was being returned. Providing that substations were interconnected by such as Hastings Couplers, it was not necessary to install such equipment in every substation. Manchester had only one load bank, at Ancoats substation, to deal with the whole of the east-side routes to Audenshaw, Denton, Haughton Green and Guide Bridge.

Because they were responsible for their own areas, both Ashton and SHMD had to make similar provision for the sections of overhead which they maintained. It has been noted that Manchester obtained retrospective operating powers for the north Manchester scheme (The 1946 Act); it goes without saying that similar powers were required

for all of the trolleybus operation in Ashton and Manchester. Time has not permitted full research into all the details of these powers (an interesting project for the student of transport who also has an interest in Parliamentary matters), but equally both Ashton and the SHMD Board, despite the latter never operating trolleybuses themselves, would have needed the appropriate primary legislation. Furthermore, once the powers had been obtained and the infrastructure put into place, it was necessary for each section to be examined by the Ministry of Transport's inspecting officer before services commenced. Any recommendations about such matters as speed over junctions or beneath overbridges would be made at that time.

It has already been noted that there was a strong desire to support local industry, and by definition, local employment, in the question of rolling stock provision. This extended no less to the provision of electrical equipment for the trolleybuses themselves. All of the Manchester vehicles, and all but four of the Ashton ones, utilised Metro-Vick equipment. The Metropolitan-Vickers Electrical Company, to give the company its full name, was based in Trafford Park, and is a subject worthy of a book in its own right. It had its origin with the British Westinghouse Electric and Manufacturing Company, a subsidiary of

Westinghouse of America, and from 1903 began to produce electrical equipment for tramways all over Britain, from premises which probably employed the largest number of people in Trafford Park at the time.

These days such a parentage would be no bar to success, but the nationalistic atmosphere brought about by the First World War was a handicap. Supported by funds from the Metropolitan Carriage, Wagon and Finance Company, British Westinghouse became exactly that. In 1919 Vickers Limited, recognising that their skills and business acumen in producing warships, tanks and guns from steel, would ideally be supplemented in peacetime conditions by involvement in the production of associated electrical equipment, took over both the Westinghouse and Metropolitan Companies and the Metropolitan-Vickers Electrical Company was born. In 1929 Metro-Vick combined with British Thomson-Houston, Ferguson Pailin and Edison Swan to form Associated Electrical Industries, but the Metro-Vick name continued in use until 1960 when the works, still in Trafford Park, became AEI (Manchester) Ltd.

At the time trolleybus operation was introduced into Manchester, Metro-Vick employed around 16,000 at its Trafford Park works. Not only did it supply the traction motors to the Crossley and

When Ashton decided in 1954 to have new bodies fitted to some of their utility trolleybuses, a not unusual step amongst trolleybus operators, their choice for the builder of the first two was a little out of the ordinary, the contract going to SH Bond of Wythenshawe, whose previous experience of this type of vehicle had been confined to the rebuilding of some of the early SLT vehicles. (STA)

Leyland chassis, but also generators, resistances, switch gear, circuit breakers and fuses.

To support the trolleybus operation on the street, both Ashton and Manchester utilised specialised vehicles for the purpose. Until 1932 Ashton used a Vulcan tower wagon to maintain the overhead, but from that year a Guy single-deck bus dating from 1925 was converted. This lasted until 1942, by which time a 1939 normal-control Bedford had been taken into stock. Initially, Manchester used retired AEC and Daimler motorbuses, which dated from the 1920's. Between 1937 and 1947 four forward-control Thornycrofts were purchased, and in 1945 a Leyland Tiger single-decker was rebuilt as a tower wagon. Finally, two new Guy Vixen tower wagons were obtained in 1957. For the sake of completeness, it should be recorded that SHMD also favoured Thornycroft, and at one time ran a Sturdy tower wagon of this make to maintain the overhead for which it had responsibility but which was used by Ashton and Manchester trolleybuses.

In carrying out the rebuilding work for SLT, one has the distinct impression that, in part, Bond's thinking was to a degree influenced by the post-war design for Ashton and Manchester's post-war Crossleys. Whilst it is not now possible to say that the windscreen sizes were identical, SLT's Guys being 7ft 6in wide, whilst the Crossleys were 8ft wide, there was undeniably a remarkable similarity in design and windscreen outline. Ashton's 78 is seen in its home town whilst SLT 20 crosses the East Lancashire Road on the long journey from Swinton to Atherton which actually had begun way back in Farnworth. *(JSK/RB)*

A New Age

King George VI died in February 1952 and the country entered a second Elizabethan age. The effects of wartime austerity had yet to be completely thrown off – there was still rationing in place – but the Coronation which was to take place in June 1953 gave the population something to anticipate. Manchester's General Manager, Albert Neal, was also looking to the future at this time. There were two major issues to be addressed. The cost of motorbus operation was increasing - even in those days the government tax on diesel fuel was contentious - and the pre-war trolleybus fleet was beginning to show signs of its age. Whilst 14 years might have been considered a reasonable age at

which to withdraw a motorbus which had spent all its life on city operation, such an age, all things being equal, was not the stage in its life when one might normally have been considering the replacement of a trolleybus. Indeed, one of its virtues, that of a relatively vibration free existence, tended to prolong body life. But all things were not equal. The trolleybus fleet had struggled on during the dark days without much, if any, of the planned maintenance that would ordinarily have been expected to take place and a decision on possible replacement was necessary.

More importantly, however, the financial arguments for and against trolleybuses were again finely balanced, with Mr Neal addressing this issue in a comprehensive report prepared by him and which was considered by the Council in April

Manchester's first BUT, with body by HV Burlingham of Blackpool, was delivered in the summer of 1955. Here, the vehicle in question, No. 1302, is shown meeting the requirement to tilt successfully to 28 degrees in a decidedly more sophisticated environment than the earlier Crossley views with blocks of wood and jacks being used to raise the vehicle. Manchester was already buying motor bus bodies from the Blackpool factory though there had been questions about the use of non-union labour and other related issues which had needed to be resolved before the contracts could be confirmed. *(RGRC)*

1953. The advantages of the trolleybus were listed as :-

    1. Electrical energy is cheaper than fuel and is home produced.

    2. Longer vehicle life and lower vehicle maintenance costs.

    3. Three-axle vehicles available, giving more seats.

    4. More rapid acceleration, smoother silent running and no exhaust fumes.

The advantages of the motorbus were listed as:-

    1. Complete mobility and availability for all services.

    2. Higher overall speeds on some types of services.

    3. Cheaper vehicle and no outlay for overhead equipment.

    4. Less traffic congestion, as vehicles are able to pass each other.

    5. No dislocation of services due to current failure or damage to wires.

    6. Does not incur rates.

    7. No unsightly overhead lines, less difficult to operate in ice and snow, and a breakdown confined to vehicle concerned.

(In relation to (6) listed above, today's reader may not appreciate that at the time of the report, a tram or trolleybus system was forced to pay rates on its overhead wiring. In relation to (7), in severe winter weather it was customary to run a vehicle all-night to keep the overhead from becoming covered in ice.)

Mr Neal also observed that in continuing the present system, cross town services would be restricted. Manchester's experience was that this type of service had been shown to generate more revenue than two independent services terminating in the city. He added that it was considered that services to new housing estates would need a frequency of 15 minutes, which was nothing like sufficient to cover the costs of overhead wiring.

Ashton too was similarly considering the future of its trolleybus fleet and advised Manchester that it wished to retain trolleybuses for at least ten years.

An interesting passage in the report, when comparing the relative costs of trolleybuses and motorbuses, indicated that for the power consumed by the six million miles per year covered by the trolleybuses, the coal needed in a modern generating plant was about 10,700 tons; the fuel needed for the same number of motorbus miles was 666,000 gallons, which would cost the country £27,000 in imports. Yet, if the coal was exported and not used for power generation, it could be sold abroad for £59,000. Thus it was, at the time, more economic for the country to buy fuel and sell coal. But that hardly helped Manchester!

The report's recommendations were accepted by Manchester's Council. These were that:-

1. Consideration of extension of the trolleybus system be deferred until the next programme of motor bus replacement was complete.

2. Sixty-two new trolleybuses be purchased.

3. Representations be made to the Government to point out the difficulty of the economic position facing the Department.

On 7th October 1953 orders were duly placed for 62 new trolleybuses. In the meantime, the final stage of the trolleybus route renumbering had taken place when, on 31st August, the 31, 32, 33 and 34 (a number that had only first appeared in the

At the time Manchester placed the order with Burlingham, the majority of the Corporation's double-deck bodies were still coming from Metro-Cammell in Birmingham, and one of these can be seen in this picture taken in Stevenson Square, as almost-new trolleybus No. 1320 passes the familiar road sweeper's appurtenances of the day, neatly parked at the kerbside and clearly having caught the Leyland photographer's eye. *(STA)*

timetable the previous year for the 33X journeys that ran out in the morning peak via Rochdale Road and in via Conran Street) became the 211, 212, 212X and 214. The 33X journeys (to Moston Lane) became 214s.

Having decided on the future of the system following the comprehensive review mentioned above it, therefore, was a little surprising to learn in September 1954 that the Moston services were being considered for replacement by motor buses. However, it has to be appreciated that the 1953 decision had only dealt with the problem of the first 76 of Manchester's trolleybuses, and now it was the turn of the 77 vehicles delivered in the early part of the war which were coming up for consideration for replacement. Again, these vehicles had suffered considerably through lack of maintenance, some never even having received

The interior views of the Burlingham trolleybus bodies show attractive moquette seating in the lower saloon and brown Rexine-covered seats in the upper saloon, moquette not being considered appropriate in an environment where smoking was still customary. *(GMTS)*

an overhaul in over ten years. In tandem with this was the requirement that the overhead would shortly require replacement. It will be remembered that unlike the Ashton Road services, where completely new equipment had been provided, the Moston services had been converted on a 'make do and mend' basis, utilising equipment which had never been intended for these services. Perhaps it is not surprising that the full Council initially referred this proposal back to its Transport Committee, but in October 1954 it was accepted.

The next few months were, therefore, perhaps not the most glorious in the history of the Moston trolleybus services. Withdrawal of not only the wartime vehicles commenced, but the remaining trolleybuses in the pre-war 1000 series also began to be withdrawn. In fact, some had already been off the road for up to two years, and the leaking bodywork of many of the others had to be seen to be believed. The electrical supply to the system, which originally had been one of the reasons for selecting the routes for conversion, now began to fail, with the result that motorbuses from all over Manchester had to be called in at short notice to cope. Motorbus substitution was in any case becoming a more frequent occurrence, in order to prepare crews for the changeover.

No less than three shiny new BUTs are seen in this scene captured in Stevenson Square in the summer of 1956. Lyons Cafe would have provided a suitable location for the photographer whilst he awaited the arrival of his quarry. (STA)

Immediately following on from the construction of 62 BUT 9611T models for Manchester, eight were built in 1956 for Ashton as seen opposite. The bodies for these were again built by Bond, singling them out as the only batch of new trolleybuses in the country to have such a builder. (STA)

Ashton Fleet Developments

Although almost every decision taken in Manchester had some effect on the Ashton system, the policy over the replacement of their rolling stock had not reflected those of their bigger brother at the other end of Ashton Road. The five Crossley trolleybuses that had entered service at the turn of 1950 were, in effect, additions to the fleet, which then totalled 34, its highest ever, without the commensurate increase in operational demand like Manchester. Such a situation undoubtedly permitted some catching up on maintenance which the war years had prevented, although the demands on the service had been considerable, to the extent, of course, that war-time utility trolleybuses had been taken into stock, which brought their own problems. The arrival of the post-war Crossleys did allow the withdrawal of two of the pre-war six-wheel Crossleys a year later, but further reductions in fleet size did not take place until October 1954 when the first two of the 1940 batch of Crossleys were taken out of service. The next development in Ashton related directly to the wartime acquisitions. Utility bodies, in general, suffered from the fact that they were constructed with less than ideal

materials, in particular the unseasoned wood, which gave rise to most problems. The greater anticipated life of a trolleybus chassis made the rebodying of such a worthwhile proposition, and many utility trolleybuses were thus given a new lease of life. One of the first operators to appreciate this was Ashton Corporation, and in December 1954 No. 64 re-appeared with a new body by SH Bond of Wythenshawe. It was necessary for it to be taken to the Edge Lane works of Liverpool Corporation in order for it to undergo its mandatory tilt test. Bonds, whilst new to the complete provision of bodywork, had rebuilt many of the pre-war trolleybus fleet of the South Lancashire Transport Company, in the process giving 1930s Guy trolleybuses a frontal appearance not unlike the post-war Crossley trolleybuses.

The sensational return of No. 64 was not so much as a result of Bond's skill, but the fact that it appeared in a brand new livery. Gone was the red, white and blue, to be replaced by Peacock blue and cream, with, for good measure, a scarlet band. This latter feature was apparently too much for the good folk of Ashton, and the new livery, which it was said was less resistant to fading and could be applied by spray painting, omitted this feature. In due course the whole of the fleet was turned out in this new colour scheme.

Abandonment Commences

The 212, 212X and 214 were chosen as the first Rochdale Road Garage services to be converted, with effect from April 1955. The replacement motorbuses were not brand new, but the changeover did permit the Corporation to initiate another stage of its move to introducing more cross city services, as the replacing 114 operated from Gardener's Arms to Sale Moor, was worked by motorbuses from Princess Road and Rochdale Road Garages, in the case of the latter, its first diesel allocation. The last trolleybus on the 214 ran on Saturday 23rd April, the last 212 operating the following day.

One of the conditions imposed on suppliers by Manchester Corporation was that when a large batch of vehicles was being delivered, the very first such unit should be supplied some time in advance of the full delivery, in order to sensibly 'iron out' any teething problems that might arise. Thus No. 1302, not numerically the first of the new trolleybuses, arrived in June 1955, some three months ahead of the rest of the delivery. It was allocated to Rochdale Road Garage, and with all the experience that Murphy's law has demonstrated to us over the years, it duly appeared on the remaining service operating to Moston, the 211, despite the fact that the service had barely two months of trolleybus operation left.

It is understood that after years of suffering a failing trolleybus fleet, the passengers from the Moston area were not best impressed (to put it politely!) with the introduction of this brand new vehicle, which was destined for operation in other parts of the city. It would seem that the Manchester management, recognising when they had scored an own goal, ensured that 1302 did not operate on the 211 again. Indeed, there was precious little time for it to do so, for the 211 along Oldham Road became the 80 motorbus (once again) from 8th August that year. Little of the overhead had been removed following the conversion of the 212 and 214, but after the 211 was replaced, removal started in earnest, although it was some months before the work was completed. At the same time, the last of the pre-war trolleybuses were taken out of service. Nearly all of the 1100-36 batch, which had always been based at Rochdale Road, were also withdrawn, with the exception of Nos. 1104 and 1133, which were transferred to Hyde Road. This was because from 24th April 1956 Rochdale Road became a purely motorbus garage. The remnants of the 1137-76 batch which were not already at Hyde Road, joined them there. Manchester's trolleybus fleet as at 31st March 1956 totalled 143 units, all of which were now to be Hyde Road based. The individual route requirement was as follows:-

210 28 trolleybuses
213 14 trolleybuses
215 23 trolleybuses
216 19 trolleybuses
217 9 trolleybuses (plus Ashton vehicles)
218 17 trolleybuses (plus Ashton vehicles)
219 28 trolleybuses (plus Ashton vehicles)

Manchester and Ashton Corporation Transport Departments.

TROLLEYBUS Service No. 217 - ASHTON AND HAUGHTON GREEN.

Commencing Monday, 4th. July 1960, this service will be converted to Motor Bus operation and will be re-numbered 127.

Times, fares and stopping places will be the same as the existing service.

Manchester's New Fleet

As indicated previously, the first of the 62 trolleybuses ordered in the autumn of 1953 had arrived in June 1955. The batch was numbered 1301-62 (at last someone in MCTD had realised numerical sequences commenced at '1' and not '0'), and were given class number 96. Thereafter, delivery was spread from September 1955 through to March 1956, at a rate of between five and eighteen per month. All were initially delivered to Rochdale Road, subsequently being transferred to Hyde Road. The order for the chassis had been placed with the British United Traction Company (BUT), which was a company jointly owned by Leyland Motors and AEC, the latter having taken Crossley over as explained earlier. The 60-seat bodies were supplied by HV Burlingham of Blackpool. It would appear that the Council was still supporting local (or at least Lancashire) industry. At the time, this company had been supplying bodies on both Daimler and Leyland

To assist those attempting to place the location we will make the task easier by advising that this bodybuilder's photograph was taken near the factory. *(RGRC)*

motorbus chassis to Manchester Corporation, and there was a distinct resemblance between the two. Burlingham had a reputation for well made bodywork, Ribble Motor Services of Preston (perhaps not surprisingly), being an important customer. They had only built one batch of trolleybuses before, however, for Portsmouth Corporation in 1952, interestingly again on BUT chassis. BUT had no premises of their own and trolleybus chassis assembly, therefore, took place at locations owned either by Leyland or AEC. In the case of this Manchester order, what could be more suitable than to use the former Crossley premises at Errwood Park. They were, in fact, the last chassis for Manchester assembled at that location.

The model supplied to Manchester was the 9612T, which was, to all intents and purposes, based on the AEC Regent motor bus chassis. Standardisation was at least achieved as far as the electrical equipment was concerned, for it was once again supplied by Metro-Vick. The batch carried registration marks ONE 701-62; the writer has always felt that it was a shame that ONE 301-62 were not obtained from the motor taxation office, which would have permitted matching fleet and registration numbers like nothing ever before or since! Apparently a motorcycle had been allocated a number in the series, so preventing it happening.

The Suez Crisis

Not wishing to be outdone by its larger neighbour, Ashton had been pursuing its vehicle modernization policy during this time. A year after No.64 had returned from SH Bond, it was the turn of No. 63 to receive the same treatment, returning to service in December 1955. Since Manchester had indicated that trolleybuses were to remain for the time being, Ashton decided that a batch of new vehicles was required. As in 1940, Ashton, therefore, took delivery of eight chassis which were identical to Manchester's recent deliveries, the chassis numbers of Ashton's BUT 9612Ts following on from the 62 Manchester ones. Obviously satisfied with the work on the rebodied utilities, SH Bond was once again favoured with the order, and the first of this batch arrived in Ashton in September 1956. Ashton was the only trolleybus operator to take trolleybuses bodied by Bond. The delivery of these trolleybuses permitted the withdrawal of the last of the pre-war trolleybuses and all but two of the 1940 deliveries.

The next development affecting the network was brought about by events far from the North West of England. The Anglo-French reaction to the nationalisation of the Suez Canal by Egypt in the summer of 1956 led ultimately to the closure of the Canal and the introduction of petrol rationing and a reduction in the availability of fuel supplies. For a short while the crisis was manna from heaven for the pro-trolleybus lobby, as the Regional Traffic Commissioners instructed bus operators to reduce mileage. Manchester's solution to the crisis was to increase trolleybus operation along Hyde Road with effect from 17th December. The 210 service was paralleled as far as Thornley Park by the jointly operated (Manchester and Salford) cross city 57/77, to which reference has been made previously. This service was split outside peak hours, and while Salford maintained motorbuses on its part of the service, Manchester introduced a new trolleybus service numbered 210X from Piccadilly to Thornley Park. The many extra journeys to Belle Vue were also covered by trolleybuses and the 57X all night service became the 210X all night service, also to Thornley Park. As a result, the 1240-55 Dominion trolleybuses saw continuous all day service. On Saturdays the football traffic on the 213 to Maine Road was covered entirely by trolleybuses, with through journeys from Guide Bridge and Audenshaw once again reverting to

trolleybus operation, the connection at Chancellor Lane, normally used for depot workings, permitting these routings. A frequent service also ran from Stevenson Square.

The same date as the introduction of the increased 210 service also saw a change in the terminal point in Piccadilly, when it was moved from George Street to outside the Queens Hotel. The trolleybus overhead at the Mosley Street end of Piccadilly and along Parker Street was, therefore, taken out of use after barely seven years, with the exception that the night service 215X continued to use this section until February 1957, when removal of the overhead saw the terminus transferred to Stevenson Square. The 'Suez Emergency' was to last until 1st April 1957, when the trolleybus 'swan song' concluded and matters reverted to those which existed four months previously. The terminus of the 218, 218X, 219 and 219X services were moved across the road in Portland Street, terminating outside the Queens Hotel from 16th June 1957. This resulted in trolleybuses on these services approaching Piccadilly via London Road and leaving via Aytoun Street, the reverse of the previous and original arrangement. The following day, certain journeys on the 219X which terminated at The Trough were moved to start in Aytoun Street and were numbered 212.

Decline

Whilst not specifically relevant to our story, for the sake of completeness and to include the dates in their correct chronological order, it should be recorded that the only other remaining trolleybus systems in Lancashire both closed in 1958, St Helens at the end of June and SLT two months later. While there still remained another 28 trolleybus operators in the country (or 27, if one counts Grimsby-Cleethorpes as one), including that of London Transport, which was by far and away the largest user, and where no contraction of the network had yet taken place, it is probably fair to say that the tide had begun to turn for the trolleybus.

Nevertheless, Ashton had completed the rebodying of two more of its utility trolleybuses in 1958, this time Nos. 61 and 62 receiving new bodies from CH Roe. This particular style of body by Roe found favour with several other operators of utility trolleybuses, including Doncaster, Maidstone, Tees-side and Wolverhampton. Derby also took the version on new chassis. In fact, it is pleasing to note that in 2006 one of the diecast model bus makers has released a model of the Tees-side example. How long before we shall see an Ashton one? On the down side, January 1959 saw the removal from Manchester's fleet of the last of the 1940 Leylands, Nos. 1104 and 1133 lasting considerably longer than the rest of their brethren. Life at Hyde Road must have been somewhat easier than their Rochdale Road duties, although it is possible that they were retained for use as driver training vehicles.

The march of progress in the city centre was the next factor to influence the future of the trolleybus system. In 1959 the Co-operative Wholesale Society completed negotiations to build a multi-storey office block at the corner of Miller Street and Corporation Street for the Co-operative Insurance Society. The site had been derelict since the war, after Herr Goering had identified it for an early urban renewal scheme. In the 21st century, with its emphasis on renewable energy, the building has been fitted with solar panels, changing considerably the appearance of this well-known CIS landmark. Clearly there were

The final stage in the modernisation of Ashton's fleet came in 1958 were the remaining two Park Royal bodied Sunbeam W chassis had new bodies fitted by CH Roe of Crossgates, Leeds. *(JSK)*

implications for the 213 service. Two alternatives were presented by the General Manager. Even today the first seems wildly inappropriate. This was to extend the service across Ducie Bridge to New Bridge Street, which was going away from the city centre; the second proposal was for the service to travel down Shude Hill and Withy Grove to Corporation Street, returning to Rochdale Road via Corporation Street. This alternative proposal did not find favour with the Police, perhaps not surprisingly, who feared dewirements in this busy area would cause chaos. Mr Neal's final recommendation was to convert the service to motorbuses, using the Withy Grove option. One is tempted to wonder whether either proposal was a serious solution to the problem, or just a smokescreen to hasten the trolleybus demise.

Now that the ball had started rolling, enabling decisions on trolleybus conversion to be made without the previous justification over the cost of replacement of either rolling stock or infrastructure, it was not long before the next candidate for consideration was identified. A new overspill estate was to be built at Haughton Green and it was considered that most of the residents would require transport into the city. Extensions and modifications to the overhead would have been necessary on the estate, and a service to Ashton was not really going to meet the new demand, even though a new service could have been provided

by trolleybuses, as the junctions already existed at Denton to permit a through route. But it seems that once it was in the mind of the 'powers-that-be' to commence abandonment, solutions to retain trolleybuses were not being sought. It was true that 27 of the 1940's delivered Crossleys were due for retirement, so the conversion of both the 213 and the 217 would aid this.

A week before the 213 conversion, a modified overhead layout at The Snipe was introduced as a result of road works and the construction of a new gyratory system, the terminal point of the 215 being moved to Lumb Lane at Ryecroft Hall, and the reverser at Gainsborough Road, the only one on the system, was removed. The new layout also permitted vehicles to turn back from the Ashton direction, although it is not known how often, if ever, this was used. The last trolleybus on the 213 ran on Sunday 31st May, the replacing motorbus service being rather cleverly numbered 123, in accordance with Manchester's policy of giving the replacement service a number similar to the one being withdrawn. Before this happened, a group of enthusiasts hired an Ashton trolleybus to visit the Miller Street section. Again, regrettably, no photographs have yet come to light illustrating this unique occurrence, nor has it so far been possible to identify the vehicle concerned.

The 217 was to last a little longer, final trolleybus journeys taking place on 3rd July 1960, the replacement motorbus service being numbered 127. The closure allowed Ashton to make further reductions in its trolleybus rolling stock; the remaining two wartime Crossleys (Nos. 51 & 54) being withdrawn for scrap and going to North's of Leeds, as had all the others of the batch. The opportunity was also taken to deal with the remaining, and newest, two utility vehicles. This time Nos. 65 & 66, whilst journeying over the Pennines (as Nos. 61 & 62 had done), were in for a one-way trip, as they were sold to Bradford City Transport. Bradford's astute General Manager, Chaceley Humpidge, had an eye for 'bargains' and paid £350 each for these two Sunbeams in September 1960 (the motors, Metro-Vick in this case, unlike Ashton's other utilities, were probably worth that alone), and they were provisionally given Bradford fleet Nos. 821/0. Parked at Bradford's Thornbury depot, their Peacock blue livery did not look out of place. It was intended that in due course they would have been fitted with new forward-entrance bodies by East Lancashire

Coachbuilders as was Bradford's policy, but the departure of Mr Humpidge the following year brought about the abandonment of such plans, although the motors were re-used.

It was to be a while before part of the justification for the conversion to motorbuses of the 217 was to be put in place, however, for no direct link to Manchester was provided for some time. But the die was cast. A new reason now existed for justifying the conversion of trolleybus routes, that of new overspill housing estates. It was not long before proposals for new housing at Hattersley, on the edge of Hyde, allowed suggestions to be made about the future of the 210 service. Ashton Corporation was obviously watching events with renewed interest. At the time of the 1953 report they had indicated that they would wish to see trolleybuses retained for at least ten years, so that when, in 1958, enquiries had been made of Manchester as to the date of any possible conversions, they had somewhat forcibly been reminded of their commitment. In forward planning terms, those ten years were soon to be reached. Talk of converting the 210 was not going to help Ashton with its planning process. Changes to road layouts, generally brought about by the increase in road traffic, also became a spur to raise the spectre of trolleybus abandonment. In Ashton's case, a new roundabout complex was planned for Chester Square.

Ashton also had plans for a new bus station in the redeveloped town centre. In both cases, it was not enamoured by the prospect of erecting new overhead which would then only exist for a less than economic life span. By the autumn of 1961 matters were coming to a head, and yet another report was commissioned by Manchester. It transpired that the trolleybus peak demand of 143 vehicles only five years before was now down to 102, although the fleet stood at 116. Obviously the removal of the 213 and 217 had reduced this figure, but traffic levels seemed to be down significantly too, as the 219 requirement had dropped from 28 to 19. It was noted that by the end of the financial year 1961/2 the debt on the oldest trolleybuses, the post-war Crossleys, would be cleared. They had received their first major overhauls in 1955/6, and would soon be due for a second. A saving on expenditure of around £900 per vehicle would arise if further abandonment were considered now. The loan taken out on the BUTs would be repaid in 1967. Further heavy expenditure on the overhead would also be avoided.

The decision made on 6th December 1961 was hardly surprising. The 1200 and 1240 classes would be replaced within two years, overhead renewals would be kept to a minimum and overhauls on the BUTs would be intended to see them last only until 1967. Both the joint operators, Ashton and SHMD, were advised accordingly. The former was not at all impressed, although it was agreed that the conversion of the 219 would be accelerated so that the work required at Chester Square could be minimised. Even without the 210 service, the maximum trolleybus requirement as indicated by the report would be 74. Since only 62 BUTs were to remain, it would seem that there was a tacit acceptance that motorbuses would have to be used on the remaining trolleybus services even then, although officially no mention of this was made. In fact, the first BUT to be withdrawn was No. 1346 in January 1962. Motorbuses 'officially' commenced operation on the 210 after 19th January 1963, in the midst of one of the most severe winters on record. Short workings to Hyde

were worked by motorbuses so that they could serve Hyde Bus Station, and the regular Saturday afternoon service to Denton, normally worked by the six-wheelers, used these vehicles for the last time that day. The spectacle of a six-wheeler turning at Denton was worth viewing, as it involved a right turn at Crown Point into Stockport Road (wiring shared with the 217 until 1960) and then three tight left hand turns via Inman Street and Saxon Street to regain Hyde Road. Almost half the six-wheelers were taken out of service as a result, and the last trolleybus of all on the service ran on 28th April 1963. Ironically it was a BUT, No. 1302, operating from Smithy Lane to Hyde Road garage. This time the replacing motorbuses used the same 210 service number.

Following this, all the remaining Crossley trolleybuses were taken out of service. The last six-wheeler ran in July, while the last of the four-wheelers lingered until October. SHMD was now only responsible for the overhead in Stalybridge, and handed charge of this over to Ashton. Thus

MOTOR TRANSPORT
LONDON. 25 JANUARY. 1963   NINEPENCE

details from:—
CLAYTON DEWANDRE CO. LTD.,
LINCOLN. ENGLAND.

THE RESCUE

SNOW WAS ONLY ONE HAZARD

DESPITE blizzards three 18ft-high sections of a welded steel-column were successfully hauled from Dukinfield to Birkenhead docks on Sunday.

The only suitable route was through Hyde, Stockport, and along the Chester by-pass. Even this involved the lifting of trolley-bus wires at two road junctions in Hyde.

The 116ft steel column, made by Daniel Adamson and Co. Ltd. for an oil refinery in Mombasa, was divided into three to facilitate transport.

The haulier carrying out the operation was Edward Beck and Son Ltd., Stockport.

Conversion of Manchester's 210 service commenced in January 1963 during a particularly severe winter. An oversize load requires the assistance of SHMD's tower wagon to negotiate the snow covered turning circle at Gee Cross. *(RGRC)*

the 210 became the shortest lived all day trolleybus service in Manchester, at thirteen years and three months, and one can only wonder at the economics of it all. Fifty-four thirteen-year-old trolleybuses, which, had they been given another overhaul, would have been good for at least another half-a-dozen years operation, were offered for scrap. Only 1250 escaped the breaker's torch and is today to be found in the Greater Manchester Museum of Transport at Boyle Street. Before the end of the year the peak hour service numbered 212 (a short working of the 219), was converted to motorbus operation. Management changes also took place at Ashton during 1963 when Terence O'Donnell left for Northampton and was replaced by Ken Griffiths, who at one time had been Rolling Stock Engineer at Bradford and before that Assistant Engineer with Liverpool, and was thus more than familiar with electric traction.

Further economies were introduced from 19th July 1964. After that date most of the Manchester trolleybus workings on service 218 were converted to motor bus operation, the all-night trolleybus working on service 215X being replaced by motorbuses at the same time. This was probably the last all-night service in the country to utilise trolleybuses. Sunday operation by trolleybuses also ceased at this time. The full 219 service followed from 10th October, and Ashton lost no time in removing its section of overhead between Guide Bridge and Chester Square. This conversion also allowed Ashton to withdraw the last of the post-war Crossleys, but unlike Manchester, where the only trolleybuses that remained in stock were the BUTs, Ashton retained the last two of its rebodied Sunbeams, which were not withdrawn until December 1965. Final vehicles on the 219 were No. 88 for Ashton and No. 1345 for Manchester, which operated the 11.28 pm journey from Guide Bridge to Hyde Road. Enthusiasts hired No. 1319 for a tour on the last day. Ashton Council must have been grateful to its neighbour for its sympathetic assistance in accelerating matters. As regards its other wishes, the simple expedient was followed by retaining the trolleybus overhead 'in situ' in the town centre and the services concerned did not enter Ashton Bus Station until after final trolleybus abandonment.

The preservation of trolleybuses was now beginning to gather pace, partly because the closure of systems was now occurring more regularly, and partly because once the first privately preserved

trolleybus had been obtained in Reading in 1961 by a pioneering group led by the late Mike Dare, others were encouraged to follow his example. Martin Ford obtained BUT No. 1344 in the same month as Manchester withdrew its vehicles from the 218. This trolleybus led a somewhat chequered existence for many years, the writer recalling seeing it parked variously at a milk depot in Hazel Grove, and later within Oldham Corporation's depot at Mumps, during the time he lived in the North West. It is to figure again in our story, but today it can be found in full working order running at the East Anglia Transport Museum at Carlton Colville near Lowestoft.

More road works, this time close to Manchester city centre, and involving the construction of what is now the A57(M), although at the time simply the 'Mancunian Way', resulted in the construction of a roundabout at Fairfield Street which necessitated revising the overhead arrangements during the summer of 1964. Further work on the Mancunian Way resulted in overhead, redundant from the 210 conversion, but still used by Hyde Road garage workings, being taken out of use along Hyde Road and at Ardwick Green in July 1965. In Ashton the long awaited work at Chester Square was progressing and the new arrangements came into use from April 1965. Despite other traffic being diverted during this time, trolleybuses continued to operate right through the road works throughout their duration.

Only the 215, 216 and 218 now remained, and only the latter saw Ashton trolleybuses as well as Manchester ones, although technically the 216 and 218 were jointly operated by Ashton, Manchester and the SHMD Board. True joint 'on the road' operation was to last only until May 1966, when Manchester converted its workings on the 218 to motorbus. In the same way that AF Neal had arrived just in time to see the trams finally withdrawn, so his successor, RF Bennett, arrived from Bolton to see the conclusion of the trolleybus withdrawal programme.

Mr Bennett's valedictory announcement came in July 1966 and stated that the final operation would take place in December that year, and the next move towards this total elimination took place at the end of August, when Saturday operation ceased and trolleybuses were only used from Mondays to Fridays. The one exception to this was an enthusiast's tour which took place on Saturday 3rd September using 1325.

As only Ashton was now operating trolleybuses on the Old Road, the opportunity was taken to remove surplus overhead at Fairfield Road and The Trough. Wiring in Newton Street and outward along London Road between Hilton Street and Fairfield Street was also taken down in November, the month that confirmation was announced that the final day would be Friday 30th December. The final evening was dry and quite a number of additional passengers, both enthusiasts and members of the general public, took the opportunity for a last ride. Virtually no ceremony was attached to the last official journeys, although Ashton 87 was decorated with posters and its last run was duplicated by 83 on the 10.30 pm departure from Piccadilly, complete with Transport Committee Chairman and General Manager in attendance. Manchester did make one small concession in providing a trolleybus on the last departure of the day on the 218X service to Audenshaw, which would normally have been a motorbus, and the final journey from Stevenson Square on the 216X to Audenshaw was also duplicated, 1353 and 1354 being used. But all of this was in dismal contrast to the arrangements for Manchester's last tram, or indeed the arrangements made on the last day of trolleybuses in London four years before. It has to be admitted that prior to the Ashton/Manchester closure such events had generally been low key, but subsequently towns such as Huddersfield, Reading and Bournemouth arranged considerable ceremony. But it was entirely in keeping with even the lifetime existence of trolleybuses in Manchester, which had never totally been welcomed of course. Now only twelve systems remained.

Reference has already been made at the beginning of this book to the final day in Manchester, which was New Year's Eve 1966. That day two trolleybuses took to the road; one the former Manchester 1344 and the other former Rotherham 37. This was probably the only time a Daimler trolleybus ran in Manchester. Fittingly 1344 had the honour of returning to Hyde Road last, and no sooner had it done so than the power was switched off and our story concluded.

The final day of joint trolleybus operation in Great Britain was Friday 30th December 1966, and Manchester 1341 prepares to turn left at Ryecroft Hall on the overhead introduced in May 1959, pursued by Ashton 87 heading for Ashton town centre and Stalybridge. *(RGR)*

Finale

As mentioned at the beginning of this book, joint running of trolleybuses by two operators was never common in the country, and with the closure of the Ashton and Manchester systems, the practice ceased. The Ashton-under-Lyne trolleybus system, for all its overshadowing by its neighbour Manchester, was nevertheless the sixth longest surviving operator in Great Britain, at 41 years. Manchester's 28 years found it eclipsed, amongst others, by Birmingham, Belfast and, of course, London. Among the handful of systems to last less than ten years, no less than three of them have formed part of this account.

On the other hand, at its maximum extent in terms of vehicles, at 171, Manchester was one of the largest ever to exist. Others did exceed this maximum figure, among which were Belfast, Glasgow and, as mentioned, London again. As we have seen, perhaps fittingly, loyalty to a local product, in the shape of the Manchester area built Crossley trolleybuses, resulted in all but two dozen of those built for United Kingdom use, belonging to either Ashton or Manchester.

Having traced the history of the two undertakings, a brief geographical survey of north, south and west Greater Manchester follows, showing the diversity of the areas served by trolleybuses.

The final day at The Snipe, the one-time terminal point of the 215 service, where a reversing triangle in the overhead existed until 1959. Greater Manchester's Metrolink may, hopefully, one day pass behind here en route to Ashton town centre, the necessary property demolition having taken place some time ago. *(RGR)*

Ashton's final trolleybus on the night of Friday 30th December 1966 was No. 87, which carried posters along the side panels recalling Ashton's 41-year association with the trolleybus. *(STA)*

A last nostalgic view of Ashton No. 87 outside Mossley Road garage on the final evening of operation. Unlike its larger neighbour Ashton's General Manager was pursuaded to mark the closure as shown below. *(JSK)*

'The morning (mourning?) after the night before'. Saturday 31st December 1966 saw Manchester's last trolleybus parked forlornly at the back of Hyde Road garage. Seldom can a last trolleybus anywhere have looked so scruffy, a reflection perhaps on the Corporation's attitude to the abandonment process. *(RGR)*

The final day of trolleybus operation in Manchester, which was down to enthusiasts, saw former BUT No. 1344 return to the overhead it had once regularly used. It was accompanied during the day by former Rotherham No. 37, a Daimler CTC6 model with Roe bodywork, a six-wheel version of that the body fitted to Ashton 61 and 62. *(RGR)*

SERVICE No. 215.—AUDENSHAW AND STEVENSON SQUARE
SERVICE No. 216.—STALYBRIDGE AND STEVENSON SQUARE
(Joint service with Ashton Corporation and S.H.M.D. Transport Board).

SUNDAY

Ashton ..dep	0535	0603	0648	..	..	0718	..	..	..	..	0803	..	..	0833	..	0848	..
Audenshaw .. ..„	0542	0610	0655	..	..	0725	..	..	..	0803	0810	0818	0833	0840	0848	0855	0903
Edge Lane .. ..„	0550	0618	0703	0713	0723	0733	0743	0753	0803	0811	0818	0826	0841	0848	0856	0903	0911
Stevenson Square ..arr	0607	0635	0720	0730	0740	0750	0800	0810	0813	0828	0835	0843	0858	0905	0913	0920	0928

Ashton ..dep	0903		03	..	18	..	33	..	48	.. mins. past	1248	..	..	1303	..	..	..
Audenshaw .. ..„	0910	then	10	18	25	33	40	48	55	03 each	1255	1300	1305	1310	1315	1320	1325
Edge Lane .. ..„	0918	at	18	26	33	41	48	53	03	11 hour	1303	1308	1313	1318	1323	1328	1333
Stevenson Square ..arr	0935		35	43	50	58	05	13	20	28 until	1320	1325	1330	1335	1340	1345	1350

Stalybridge .. ..dep			1333	then	03	..	18	..	33	..	48	..	minutes past	1448	..	..
Ashton .. ..„	..	..	1340	at	10	15	20	25	30	35	40	45	50	55	00	05 each	1455	1500	1505
Audenshaw .. ..„	1330	1335	1348		18	23	28	33	38	43	48	53	58	03	08	13 hour	1503	1508	1513
Edge Lane .. ..„	1338	1343	1405		35	40	45	50	55	00	05	10	15	20	25	30 until	1520	1525	1530
Stevenson Square ..arr	1355	1400															

Stalybridge .. ..dep	1455	..	..	1510	..		10	..	..	25	..	..	40	..	..	55	..	..	minutes
Ashton .. ..„	1502	..	..	1517	..	then	17	..	..	32	..	..	47	..	..	02	..	..	past
Audenshaw .. ..„	1509	1514	1519	1524	1529	at	24	29	34	39	44	49	54	59	04	09	14	19 each
Edge Lane .. ..„	1517	1522	1527	1532	1537		32	37	42	47	52	57	02	07	12	17	22	27 hour
Stevenson Square ..arr	1534	1539	1544	1549	1554		49	54	59	04	09	14	19	24	29	34	39	44 until

Stalybridge .. ..dep	2210	..	..	2225	..	..	..	..	..	..	..	..	..	..	..	..
Ashton .. ..„	2217	..	2225	2232	..											
Audenshaw .. ..„	2224	2229	2232	2234	2239	2239	2244	2251	2256	2301	..	2306	..	2311	2316	2326	..
Edge Lane .. ..„	2232	2236	2240	2242	2247	2247	2252	2259	2304	2309	2312	2314	2316	2319	2324	2334	..
Every Street .. ..„	..	..	..	2255	2300	2300	2305	2312	2317	2322	2325	2327	2329	2332	2337	2347	..
Stevenson Square ..arr	2249	2253	2257	..	..	..	..	..	..	..	..	..	..	..	..	..

Extracts from a mid-1960s Manchester Corporation timetable indicate that even on Sundays the frequency of services 215 and 216 was every five minutes. Interestingly the timetable refers to the joint operation between Manchester, Ashton and SHMD, even though the latter two provided no vehicles. *(RGRC)*

SERVICE No. 215.—AUDENSHAW AND STEVENSON SQUARE
SERVICE No. 216.—STALYBRIDGE AND STEVENSON SQUARE
(Joint service with Ashton Corporation and S.H.M.D. Transport Board).

SUNDAY

Stevenson Square ..dep	0458	0526	0605	0638	..	..	0723	0731	0746	0753	0801		01	08	16	23	31	38	46	53
Pollard Street .. ..„	..	..	..	..	0657	0707	..	..	..	..	..	then	..	..	..	..	..	..	..	..
Edge Lane .. ..„	0515	0543	0622	0655	0712	0722	0740	0748	0803	0810	0818	at	18	25	33	40	48	55	03	10
Audenshaw .. ..„	0523	0551	0630	0703	..	..	0748	0756	0811	0818	0826		26	33	41	48	56	03	11	18
Ashton ..arr	0530	0558	0637	0710	..	..	0755	..	..	0825	..		40	..	55	..	10	..	25

Stevenson Square ..dep	minutes	1238	1246	1253	1303	1308	1313	1318	1323	1328	1333	1338	1343	1348	1353	1358
Edge Lane .. ..„	past	1255	1303	1310	1320	1325	1330	1335	1340	1345	1350	1355	1400	1405	1410	1415
Audenshaw .. ..„	each	1303	1311	1318	1328	1333	1338	1343	1348	1353	1358	1403	1408	1413	1418	1423
Ashton .. ..„	hour	1310	..	1325	..	1340	..	..	1355	..	..	1410	..	..	1425	..
Stalybridge .. ..arr	until	..	..	..	..	..	..	..	..	..	..	..	..	..	..	..

Stevenson Square ..dep	1403	1408		03	08	13	18	23	28	33	38	43	48	53	58	minutes	2138	2143	2148
Edge Lane .. ..„	1420	1425	then	20	25	30	35	40	45	50	55	00	05	10	15	past	2155	2200	2205
Audenshaw .. ..„	1428	1433	at	28	33	38	43	48	53	58	03	08	13	18	23	each	2203	2208	2213
Ashton .. ..„	..	1440		40	..	..	55	..	..	10	..	..	25	..	hour	2210	..	..
Stalybridge .. ..arr	..	1447		47	..	..	02	..	..	17	..	..	32	..	until	2217	..	..

Stevenson Square ..dep	2153	2158	2203	2208	2213	2218	2224	2230	2235	2240	2245	2250	2254	2258	2300	..	..
Edge Lane .. ..„	2210	2215	2220	2225	2230	2235	2239	2247	2252	2257	2302	2307	2311	2315	2317	..	..
Audenshaw .. ..„	2218	2223	2228	2233	2238	2243	2247	2255	2300	2305	2310	2315	..	..	2325	..	..
Ashton ..arr	2225	..	..	..	..	..	..	..	..	..	..	..	..	..	..	..	..

In our brief review of the 210 service, we commence our journey in Piccadilly. The original terminus of the service was in George Street, a thoroughfare which disappeared in the blitz, the other end of Piccadilly from the Ashton Old Road services. The 125 motor bus service jointly operated by Manchester Corporation, North Western and SHMD to Glossop also departed from here. *(GMTS)*

Both the types of trolleybus most associated with the 210 are seen here at the Portland Street terminus outside the Queen's Hotel, to which point the 210 was moved in 1956. Salford's service 15 to Worsley terminated here and the PTE would later move its offices into the corner of the building. *(STA)*

Following the moving of the terminal point, after leaving Piccadilly the 210 utilised Whitworth Street to reach London Road, and is seen here passing the magnificent architecture that was Manchester's central fire station, and which was across the road from London Road (later Piccadilly) main line railway station. *(STA)*

Heading back into central Manchester, Crossley No. 1211 is seen here at Ardwick Green, having passed Manchester's Ardwick Hippodrome, seen in the background. Here the 210 crossed the 213 service, a situation which only lasted for nine years. The park on the left remains to this day an oasis of peace and greenery, in this little known but busy corner of the city. *(STA)*

Belle Vue was an important location on the 210 route, encompassing during the life of trolleybus service, various attractions such as a fun-fair, whose best-known feature, however, was perhaps the Bobs, a zoo, and greyhound stadium. Trolleybuses from both directions were able to turn here but in this view we see an enthusiasts' tour on the 26th June 1960 negotiating various obstacles. *(JSK)*

The long straight sections of the A57 between Manchester and Hyde were well suited to the operation of trolleybuses. One feature worthy of attention below is the Bundy clock (invented by Harlow E Bundy c1885) fixed to the pole carrying the bus stop flag (and the overhead as well, of course!). Conductors had to register their time at these points in order to provide a record of departure time. Woe betide any crew running early! *(PT)*

The section of the A57 passing by Denton golf course was, and is, a well-known speed trap for motorists, but well-suited to the operation of trolleybuses. The above view shows three-axle 1220 on the once wide-open panorama of this trunk road, now an almost entirely built up area. *(GL)*

Another view of Crossley 1210 on the enthusiasts' tour in June 1960, seen below, visited the Smithy Lane short-working of service 210. A further picture of this tour showing the participants can be seen on page 95. The Smithy Lane terminal point tended to be used by early morning journeys from Manchester as well as those at the end of the operating day. *(JSK)*

On 5th August 1962 Peter Thompson paid a visit to Hyde to photograph the 210 trolleybus service during its last summer of operation. In the upper view No. 1204 is turning off the A560 Mottram/Woodhead Road into Stockport Road, heading towards Hyde town centre. In the lower view, the first post-war Crossley, No. 1201, is travelling in the opposite direction towards Gee Cross. Above a Ford Popular carefully negotiates the corner whilst below the trend-setting Ford Anglia, with its reverse rake rear window, has now made its appearance. Less obvious is its very welcome fourth gear! *(PT- both)*

Both types of post-war Crossley trolleybus are seen here at Gee Cross. In the upper picture Empire No. 1219 is the last of Peter Thompson's three August 1962 views; the lower view shows one of the larger Dominions making the difficult manoeuvre. This turning loop was to prove to be 'a turn too far' for both types when new, as the steering geometry was far from satisfactory on them, being politely described as 'heavy'; in the canteen at Hyde Road a more basic description was undoubtedly applied. It fell to a technical assistant then with MCTD by the name of Geoffrey Hilditch to improve their performance. *(PT/JSK)*

A variety of English Electric-bodied Leylands illustrate the north Manchester services. The terminus of the 212 service was in Church Street, which runs parallel to Piccadilly. The soot-blackened buildings in the background were typical of most northern cities in the days before clean air acts were introduced; decades of industrial grime was further exacerbated by the fires from the blitz, of course. *(JAS)*

The fact that Crossley No. 1163 in this Stevenson Square view is displaying service '31' on its route blinds, whereas the unknown vehicle to the right is actually displaying '215', indicates that this photograph was taken during the early 1950s when the trolleybus service renumbering scheme was in the throes of transition. *(RM)*

After leaving the city centre, the 212 service met the 211 from Stevenson Square at Ben Brierley, whence both services ran along Moston Lane, where this picture was taken, to the terminus at The Gardener's Arms. Number 1109 is seen shortly before the service was withdrawn. Note the nearside windscreen draught excluder. *(JAS)*

Seen here on Moston Lane working the 211 service, Leyland No. 1116 has travelled from the city terminus along Oldham Road through Miles Platting before it will eventually terminate at Moston. (JAS)

Ben Brierley was an important short working on both the Rochdale Road and Oldham Road services. Crossley No.1013, one of the original batch of trolleybuses, would be withdrawn just a few weeks before service 211X too would disappear. (JAS)

A vital wartime extension was to AV Roe's at Greengate, where a large bus station existed to deal with the needs of the many workers at this aircraft factory as seen above, which includes no less than eight trolleybuses waiting to deal with the evening peak traffic. The trolleybuses, whilst in the minority compared with the motor bus specials, used the location up to 1955. Crossley No. 1176, numerically the last of the pre-war orders, stands outside the works premises on an enthusiasts tour in the lower view. *(STA; JAS)*

The 30 service was extended to Corporation Street from Rochdale Road in July 1948, becoming renumbered 213 in April 1952. BUT No.1359 is seen in Maye Street, where the actual terminal stand was situated, in this May 1959 view, just weeks before the service was converted to motorbus operation. *(JSK)*

After travelling along Great Ancoats Street, which the service shared with the 215 and 216, the 213 crossed the Ashton Old Road services. This view was taken from the corner of Pin Mill Brow and Ashton Old Road. The 213 service ran from left to right across the picture, Fairfield Street being in the background. Cartographer John Gillham was recording the layout for his overhead map. *(JCG)*

Another view of this busy junction views it from Pin Mill Brow, looking across the overhead for the Ashton Old Road services. It was taken, like the previous picture, in conditions some cynics might describe as typical Manchester weather. John Gillham probably welcomed it since it showed the overhead to good advantage. *(JCG)*

The 213 service continued past the University and through Moss Side. BUT No. 1357 is seen turning from Hart Road into Platt Lane at the southern-most extremity of the system. *(JSK)*

Before the BUTs arrived, almost every other type of Manchester trolleybus could be seen operating on this service to south Manchester, particularly on Match days when all available stock was pressed into service. Number 1149 is seen in this 1955 view along with Daimler motor bus 4135. Sister vehicle 4127 is preserved. Crossley No. 1207 was also captured by Ray Dunning the previous year at the terminal point. Ray, then a driver with MCTD, was later to become archivist to the Manchester Tramway Museum Society whose base is in Heaton Park, and, until his untimley death, was a regular driver on preserved tram 765. *(RD both)*

The Ashton New Road services had their city terminus in Stevenson Square. Leyland TTB4 No. 1063 waits to depart on the regular short-working service to Edge Lane. *(JAS)*

Seen further along the Square, Crossley TDD6 No. 1060 waits, with poles lowered, outside what was once one of many 'Joe Lyons' tea shops. *(JAS)*

BUT No.1316 has just turned into Great Ancoats Street from Oldham Street, also operating on the all-day 215X service to Edge Lane. Wiring for the 213 service came in from Oldham Road on the right. The overhead layout at this junction was considerably simplified after the closure of the north Manchester services. *(STA)*

For many years one of the landmarks on Great Ancoats Street was the art deco Daily Express building, with its extensive glass frontage. The unique style of the edifice ensured its survival, which was converted into flats. Trolleybuses on services 213, 215 and 216 were all reflected in the glazing at one time. *(STA)*

Returning from Stalybridge on its way to Stevenson Square, No. 1019 travels along Stamford Street, Ashton followed by one of the local Corporation's Crossley motor buses. *(GLC)*

Parked cars start to make their presence felt as the end of the system approaches. Number 85 leaves Ashton town centre bound for Stalybridge. *(JSK)*

In the upper view a Manchester BUT passes Stamford Park, used as a background by Ashton for some of its official views (see page 59) as it approaches Chester Square, where it will branch right for Ashton New Road. In the picture below, the first of a series taken in Stalybridge, Ashton 50 approaches its terminal point. This trolleybus was withdrawn in 1956 some three years prior to the opening of Stalybridge bus station, and is thus operating through the town in a clockwise direction. *(JSK/NDC)*

The Greater Manchester trolleybus scene at a glance. All three operators pictured (Ashton, Manchester and SHMD) obtained trolleybus powers, but only the SHMD Board, whose Daimler motorbus is seen operating on service 4, did not actually operate them. Nevertheless the overhead in this view of Stalybridge Bus Station was the Board's responsibility. *(STA)*

The terminus of both the 216 and 218 was in Stalybridge. Until November 1959 vehicles travelled via Waterloo Road and Market Street, but from that date Stalybridge bus station was opened and the loop became anti-clockwise. *(JSK)*

Immediately on leaving the bus station, trolleybuses turned into Waterloo Road. No.1342 commences its eight mile journey back to Stevenson Square. Note the feeder wires in the overhead. *(STA)*

Also in Waterloo Road, a stranger in the camp! Crossley Dominion No. 1242, working a private tour, is found far from its normal haunts on the 210 service. The post-war Crossley trolleybuses never normally operated to Stalybridge. *(GMTS)*

Before leaving Stalybridge, the trolleybus services passed along Rassbottom Street and under the lines of the former Lancashire & Yorkshire Railway at Stalybridge Station. *(STA)*

As the trolleybuses climbed out of Stalybridge, with the hills of Longdendale in the background, they passed from Cheshire into Lancashire, at which point responsibility for overhead maintenance passed from the SHMD Board to Ashton Corporation. *(JSK)*

Ashton Market Place was one of the busiest locations on the joint trolleybus network. The through line in Bow Street permitted uninterrupted passage for the Stalybridge services (Nos. 216 and 218), whilst the terminating services (Nos. 217 and 219) were able to use the loop. Numerically the last Manchester trolleybus, No. 1362, waits to depart to Haughton Green, whilst one of the two Ashton Sunbeams rebodied by Bond waits behind it. *(RB)*

For ten years Crown Point, Denton, saw the 210 and 217 services crossing at this busy junction. Ashton 54 (ETE814) heads back to its home town. A sign of changing times here as motor traffic starts to build up; two Morris Minors battle for space with a Series 2 Standard Vanguard as they approach the traffic lights in the opposite direction. The age of the working man having his own private transport has arrived. *(GL)*

With the complex overhead layout at Crown Point in Denton in the background, and a Manchester tower wagon in attendance effecting repairs, Manchester 1329 is seen at the same stop the Ashton vehicle in the previous picture. *(GL)*

The 217 service was host to all types of Ashton vehicle, and a Roe utility Sunbeam W was providing one of the schedule in this view. *(GL)*

A week before the 217 service was converted to motor bus operation, Crossley No. 1210 visited Haughton Green on an enthusiasts' tour. *(JSK)*

The participants of the tour, which included most of the-then usual suspects amongst whom were Roy Brook, Dennis Gill, Stanley King, Brian Parkin, Cliff Taylor, Ralph Jackson, Gwynne Thomas and Stan Heaton, are seen here in the 'official' group photograph with 1210 in the background. *(RB)*

Ashton 49, the original demonstrator, in original livery, stands across the road from the conveniently located local at the Haughton Green Terminus. Note the traditional bus stop fare stage plate on the standard supporting the overhead. *(RM)*

Trolleybuses from both operators are seen at Haughton Green, a fairly quiet backwater on the network. The following day, both might be found in the bustling traffic of Manchester city centre, depending on the allocation roster. *(GL)*

From the inauguration of the Ashton Old Road services in March 1938 until June 1957, the terminal point on Portland Street was adjacent to Piccadilly Gardens. This view was taken sometime between December 1956 and the following June, as the 210 service is already using its new stand outside the Queens Hotel. *(STA)*

For a short distance three parallel lines of overhead were provided for the origin 218 and 219 services by the side of Piccadilly Gardens. Manchester 1013 hides behind Ashton 64, recently rebodied by Bond. *(JSK)*

Portland Street as most people who can remember the trolleybuses in Manchester will recall it. Ashton 89 on the 218 heads Manchester 1329 on the 219. The Bedford coach is passing the bottom of Newton Street. *(JSK)*

Roe bodied Sunbeam No. 64 on service 218 turns into Aytoun Street, passing the 210 stand, following the conversion of the latter to motorbus operation. *(JSK)*

Until 1956 all services leaving Piccadilly travelled along Downing Street into London Road out of the city centre. To accommodate the introduction of a gyratory system around Piccadilly Gardens the terminal arrangements were changed from a clockwise direction to an anti-clockwise one. London Road and Piccadilly were then used in an inwards direction only. One of the Ashton Sunbeams, rebodied by Roe, finds itself on the by then redundant overhead in Piccadilly near Newton Street (probably on a tour), and one can only guess how it arrived there. Presumably it did so via Great Ancoats Street and Newton Street, neither road normally used by Ashton vehicles! *(STA)*

April 1959 found Manchester No.1165 on training duties, and it is seen here in Whitworth Street about to enter London Road, at the time this name being used for what is now Piccadilly Station. Overhead here was originally erected as an emergency alternative to Piccadilly, but Whitworth Street was also used for peak hour extras on the 210X, 218X and 219X services, which displayed 'London Road' as their destination. *(PT)*

About to pass under the second railway over-bridge in Fairfield Street, Ashton all-Crossley No. 80 (now preserved in the Manchester Museum of Transport at Boyle Street) has almost completed its journey from Stalybridge. Out of sight above and to the right is the closed Mayfield Station, still considered as a possibility for reopening to ease the load on Piccadilly's busy platforms. *(STA)*

Passing through Higher Openshaw, Ashton 78 overtakes an Austin A35 saloon, the Mini's direct ancestor. The shop blinds are out to keep the sun from fading the goods in windows and give some shade to browsing passers-by. Verily, it doesn't always rain in Manchester. *(GL)*

Manchester 1320 approaches Audenshaw parcels office and the Manchester boundary in the upper view on the 219 service in this April 1964 view, just six months before the conversion of the service to motor buses. *(PT)*

Manchester 1309 stands at the Audenshaw terminal point at Ryecroft Hall, below, introduced in 1959 and used by the 215 and 218X services. In later years there was a large filling station here; this was demolished to make way for the temporary Metrolink terminus yet to be built. *(STA)*

This view at Audenshaw in the upper picture shows BUTs of both operators, Ashton's 87 operating on the 216 from Stalybridge whilst Manchester 1335 has just turned at this point, as shown in the lower picture on the previous page, and will in due course follow the Ashton vehicle to Piccadilly. Below both Manchester vehicles have terminated at Audenshaw, and will now return to the city centre. Number 1318 in front, on the 215 service, is in the revised livery while No.1332 behind, on the 218X service, is still in the original version. The change was introduced, like so many modifications around this period, to reduce costs. *(STA/JSK)*

The 218 shown above, about to pass a Ford Consul 375, is at Chester Square where the 218 and 219 services rejoined each other, and where the overhead commenced following separate streets through Ashton town centre. *(JSK)*

This somewhat less than perfect shot has been included for the fact that it was taken on the final day of the 219 service on 10th October 1964. The motor bus behind, on the 127 service, is operating on the replacement for the 217 trolleybus route. *(PT)*

Survivors

There are just four surviving vehicles from the two fleets, the Manchester Burlingham-bodied BUT number 1344 seen here, together with its Ashton colleague Bond-bodied BUT No. 87. The former has been restored to full working order and can now be seen – and ridden – at the Carlton Colville Museum. The latter is owned by the London Trolleybus Preservation Society.

The other two survivors can be found in the Greater Manchester Museum of Transport in Boyle Street, Manchester. Three-axle Crossley Dominion number 1250 from the city's fleet has been cosmetically restored and serves as a fine reminder of the size and capacity of these vehicles. Ashton's example is of the two-axle Empire version, number 80, and both these vehicles carry Crossley bodywork. The Ashton example is presently undergoing long-term restoration but is on display with its Manchester neighbour in the upper hall of the museum.

Ashton number 80 before restoration work began. *(GMTS)*

Manchester 1250 on display in Manchester's Heaton Park to celebrate 90 years of buses in the city. *(JAS)*

Manchester 1344 operating at the Black Country Museum with a selection of other preserved vehicles in 2004. *(JAS)*

Colour pictures of Ashton trolleybuses in their red, white and blue livery have proved to be somewhat elusive and pre-war examples even more so. In the picture above, Ashton 49, the original Crossley TDD4 demonstrator, approaches Piccadilly from Aytoun Street, while below Ashton 78, one of the only five post-war trolleybuses to be delivered in this far more attractive livery, is captured in Stamford Street, Ashton, on what appears to be a quiet Summer Sunday. *(JC/GL)*

Manchester 1174, one of the last of the wartime deliveries to enter service in November 1942, is found within the Hyde Road complex near the end of its life, waiting to take up duties. Note the grey roof, which was introduced during the war. *(GL)*

An earlier example of the same batch, No. 1108, is pictured in Ashton heading back to Stevenson Square on the Stalybridge service. Yates Wine Lodge would no doubt have provided a very comfortable wating room for some, at least, of the would-be passengers though not at 5pm in those days! *(GL)*

Anyone coming across Ashton 54 could have little doubt about the activity in which it was engaged. In the view above it waits for its next trainee outside Mossley Road depot. On the occasion seen below it is about to be used in revenue service, and is seen outside the depot in company with Manchester 1315. A spare Manchester trolleybus was frequently to be found at this location. Manchester Crossley No.1231, seen opposite, complete with original style of fleet number is at the terminus used by the 210 service from its introduction in 1950 until removal to Portland Street in 1957 *(GL – all)*

The busy 210 service was the regular haunt of the 16 post-war three-axle Crossleys. In the picture above No. 1245 is passing under the Thornley Park short working facility returning to the city centre; below No. 1254 heads for Denton on a 210X working, passing two Salford vehicles laying over at the Thornley Park terminus of the joint 57 motorbus service. During the Suez crisis additional trolleybus journeys were operated to this point, at the expense of the joint motorbus service to reduce fuel oil consumption. Opposite, at the same location, one of the four-wheel post-war Crossleys, No. 1222, is operating on the full service to Gee Cross, pursued by an all-Leyland PD2 also on the 57 service. *(GL – all)*

A pictorial review of the Gee Cross terminus, who's turning loop lay across the busy A57 trunk road, is shown here. Above the first of the post-war trolleybuses, No. 1200, is seen waiting for its departure time just short of the loop, while below it is about to complete the turn. Opposite No. 1202 is seen waiting at the actual terminal point. *(GL – all)*

Ashton's post-war policy included the rebodying of some of the wartime utility deliveries. Sunbeam W Number 62 received its new Roe body in 1957, and in the interior view of the depot both the Roe bodied Sunbeams may be seen in company with a wartime Guy motor bus which has received similar treatment. *(GL – both)*

A last look at Ashton's depot above, finds two of the post-war Crossleys in their final livery parked outside. Below Manchester 1214 emerges from Hyde Road depot into Devonshire Street to take up work on peak hour service 212X, which, as the destination blind shows, terminated in Aytoun Street. Prior to June 1957 these journeys were numbered 218X or 219X, and the 212 was the only example of Manchester using the same service number for two different trolleybus services. In later years an ivory tower was built here . . . now a self-storage facility. How are the mighty fallen? *(GL – both)*

As Ashton 85 above, operating on the 218 service, passes under the overhead at Audenshaw, The Trough, it is apparent how this terminal point for service 219X acquired its name. Sister vehicle 88 is seen below on the 219 service which operated via Guide Bridge, which location is shown opposite as Manchester 1311 passes under the overhead at this point when operating on service 217 towards Ashton. The wiring layout here permitted short working vehicles to turn from any direction, whilst the scissors junction immediately above 1311 was unique on the system. *(GL – all)*

Manchester 1225 above, passes under the railway bridge in Manchester Road, Hyde where the overhead was the responsibility of the SHMD Board and whose tower wagon may be seen beyond the Crossley trolleybus. Below two Manchester BUTs are seen at Audenshaw. The nearest, No. 1338, is operating on the 215 service and will shortly turn right to return to the City via Ashton New Road. It is in the original livery for these vehicles, while No. 1342 on the 218X service behind, has recently been repainted into the simpler style. *(GL – both)*

A final view of one of Manchester's BUTs as No. 1310, in its original livery. approaches Ashton town centre on the 216. It is being pursued by a BMC Mini van, one of their most popular products, partly becuase of the low initial cost of under £400 – and not being subject to purchase tax. *(GL)*

The last day of trolleybus operation in Manchester on Saturday 31st December 1966 saw just two trolleybuses on the road. Besides Manchester's No. 1344, privately preserved Rotherham No. 37, a Daimler CTM6 rebodied by Roe, is seen together with some of its passengers at the Audenshaw loop. *(RGC)*

Ashton & Manchester Trolleybus Routes

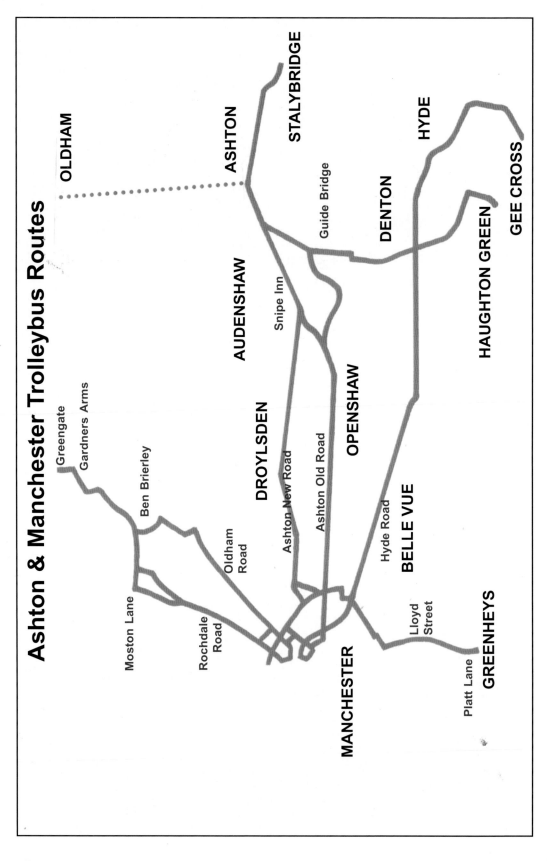

Use of Service Numbers

14	1925 - 1939	Ashton - Hathershaw - Oldham
17	1947 - 1950	Ashton - Guide Bridge - Denton - Haughton Green
26	1938 - 1950	Stevenson Square - Ashton New Road - Ashton - Stalybridge
27	1938 - 1950	Stevenson Square - Ashton New Road - Audenshaw
28	1938 - 1950	Piccadilly - Ashton Old Road - Ashton - Stalybridge
29	1939 - 1950	Piccadilly - Ashton Old Road - Guide Bridge
30	1940 - 1952	Corporation Street - University - Fallowfield
31	1938 - 1948	Piccadilly - Ashton Old Road - Audenshaw
31	1948 - 1953	Stevenson Square - Miles Platting - Moston
32	1941 - 1953	Church Street - Collyhurst - Moston
33	1941 - 1953	Church Street - Collyhurst - Moston
34	1952 -1953	Stevenson Square - Collyhurst - Moston Lane
36	1941 - 1948	Stevenson Square - Miles Platting - Moston
37	1941 - 1941	Stevenson Square - Miles Platting - Moston
55	1940 - 1941	Stevenson Square - Collyhurst -Moston Lane
57	1940 - 1947	Ashton - Guide Bridge - Denton - Haughton Green
210	1950 - 1963	Piccadilly - Denton - Hyde - Gee Cross
211	1953 - 1955	Stevenson Square -Miles Platting - Moston
212	1953 - 1955	Church Street - Moston
212	1957 - 1963	Aytoun Street - Ashton Old Road - Audenshaw
213	1952 - 1959	Corporation Street - University - Fallowfield
214	1953 - 1955	Church Street - Moston
215	1950 - 1966	Stevenson Square - Ashton New Road - Ashton - Stalybridge
216	1950 - 1966	Stevenson Square - Ashton New Road - Ashton - Stalybridge
217	1950 - 1960	Ashton - Guide Bridge - Denton - Haughton Green
218	1950 - 1966	Piccadilly - Ashton Old Road - Ashton - Stalybridge
219	1950 - 1964	Piccadilly - Ashton Old Road - Guide Bridge – Ashton

The above list is intended to show when the various service numbers were in use.
It does not imply that a particular service served all the points shown throughout its duration.

Full details of the development of the services are included in the text.

Ashton-under-Lyne Corporation Transport

Trolleybus Fleet List
1925-1966

Fleet No.	Reg. No.	Chassis	Chassis No.	Body	Seating

1925

Fleet No.	Reg. No.	Chassis	Chassis No.	Body	Seating
50	TD2362	Railless LFT30	?	Short	B36C
51	TD2497	Railless LFT30	?	Short	B36C
52	TD3147	Railless LFT30	?	Short	B36C
53	TD3148	Railless LFT30	?	Short	B34C
54-55	TD3207-08	Railless LFT30	?	Short	B36C
56	TD3262	Railless LFT30	?	Short	B36C
57	TD3344	Railless LFT30	?	Short	B36C

Nos. 50-57 rebuilt and re-seated to B34R between 1932 and 1936.
Withdrawn 1937 (52, 54), 1939 (50, 51, 53, 55-57).

1937

Fleet No.	Reg. No.	Chassis	Chassis No.	Body	Seating
48	CTD547	Leyland TTB5	14194	English Electric	H36/30R
49	CTD787	Crossley TDD4	92401	MCCW/ Crossley	H28/26R
52	CTD548	Leyland TB5	14195	English Electric	H30/24R
55	CTD549	Leyland TB5	14196	English Electric	H30/24R

Withdrawn 1953 (49), 1956 (48, 52, 55).

1938

Fleet No.	Reg. No.	Chassis	Chassis No.	Body	Seating
46-47	CTF313-314	Crossley TDD6	92314-15	MCCW/ Crossley	H38/30R
58	CNE474	Crossley TDD6	92301	MCCW/ Crossley	H38/30R

No. 58 operated on hire from 1936 to 1938 (new 1936).
Withdrawn 1951 (46-47), 1955 (58).

1940

Fleet No.	Reg. No.	Chassis	Chassis No.	Body	Seating
50-51	ETE811-812	Crossley TDD4	92490-91	MCCW/ Crossley	H28/26R
53-54	ETE813-814	Crossley TDD4	92492-93	MCCW/ Crossley	H28/26R
56-57	ETE815-816	Crossley TDD4	92494-95	MCCW/ Crossley	H28/26R
59-60	ETE817-818	Crossley TDD4	92496-97	MCCW/ Crossley	H28/26R

Withdrawn 1954 (56, 57, 59), 1956 (50, 53, 60), 1960 (51, 54).

Ashton-under-Lyne Corporation Transport

Trolleybus Fleet List
1925-1966

Fleet No.	Reg. No.	Chassis	Chassis No.	Body	Seating

1944

Fleet No.	Reg. No.	Chassis	Chassis No.	Body	Seating
61-64	FTE645-648	Sunbeam W	50083-84/ 89-90	Park Royal	H30/26R

Nos. 61-62 re-bodied by Roe to H33/28R in 1957.
No. 63 re-bodied by Bond to H33/28R in 1955.
No. 64 re-bodied by Bond to H33/28R in 1954.
Withdrawn 1963 (63, 64), 1965 (61, 62).

1946

Fleet No.	Reg. No.	Chassis	Chassis No.	Body	Seating
65	FTJ401	Sunbeam W	50324	Roe	H30/26R
66	FTJ400	Sunbeam W	50325	Roe	H30/26R

Withdrawn 1960 (65, 66).

1950

Fleet No.	Reg. No.	Chassis	Chassis No.	Body	Seating
77-81	LTC771-775	Crossley TDD42	94439-43	Crossley	H30/26R

Withdrawn 1963 (77-79, 81), 1964 (80).

1956

Fleet No.	Reg. No.	Chassis	Chassis No.	Body	Seating
82-89	YTE821-828	BUT 9612T	9612T247-54	Bond	H32/28R

Withdrawn 1966 (82-89).

Ashton's first trolleybuses arrived in 1925 and number 52 is seen here on test. When they entered service the description 'trackless trams' was more universal. In the background is one of the Corporations's trams which were soon to be replaced. *(STA)*

Manchester Corporation Transport

Trolleybus Fleet List
1938-1966

Fleet No.	Reg. No.	Chassis	Chassis No.	Body	Seating

1938

Fleet No.	Reg. No.	Chassis	Chassis No.	Body	Seating
1000-1027	DXJ951-978	Crossley TDD4	92402-29	Crossley	H28/26R
1028-1037	DXJ979-988	Leyland TB4	13611-20	Crossley	H28/30R
1050-1054	DXJ989-993	Crossley TDD6	92302-06	Crossley	H38/30R
1055-1061	ENB175-181	Crossley TDD6	92307-13	Crossley	H38/30R
1062-1087	ENB182-207	Leyland TTB4	13600-10/ 15885-99	Crossley	H38/30R

All the Crossley-built bodies were on MCCW frames.
Withdrawn 1950 (1055, 1061, 1064, 1066, 1073, 1078, 1080, 1082, 1085-1086), 1951 (1033, 1035, 1051, 1056, 1059, 1067, 1071, 1077, 1081, 1083), 1952 (1072), 1953 (1016, 1076), 1954 (1003, 1017, 1029, 1031, 1036-1037, 1065), 1955 (1000-1002, 1004-1005, 1007-1008, 1010-1014, 1020-1022, 1028, 1030, 1032, 1034, 1053, 1068-70, 1075, 1084, 1087), 1956 (1006, 1009, 1015, 1018-1019, 1023-1027, 1050, 1052, 1054, 1057-1058, 1060, 1062-1063, 1074, 1079).

1940

Fleet No.	Reg. No.	Chassis	Chassis No.	Body	Seating
1100-1136	GNA18-54	Leyland TB5	303431-67	English Electric	H28/26R
1137-1149	GNA55-67	Crossley TDD4	92450/52/53/ 51/54-59/61	Crossley	H28/26R
1150-1166	GNA68-84	Crossley TDD4	92462/60/ 63-67/69/68/ 70-79	Crossley	H28/26R

All the Crossley-built bodies were on MCCW frames.
Withdrawn 1953 (1139), 1954 (1105, 1119, 1129-1130, 1138), 1955 (1100-1101, 1106-1108, 1110-1111, 1113-1114, 1118, 1120, 1122-1124, 1128, 1135-1137, 1140-1141, 1144-1145, 1155, 1160), 1956 (1102-1103, 1109, 1112, 1115-1117, 1121, 1125-1127, 1131-1132, 1134, 1142-1143, 1146, 1149, 1154, 1157), 1958 (1158), 1959 (1104, 1133, 1147-1148, 1150-1153, 1156, 1159, 1161-1164), 1960 (1165-1166).

1941

Fleet No.	Reg. No.	Chassis	Chassis No.	Body	Seating
1167-1171	GNA85-89	Crossley TDD4	92480-84	Crossley	H28/26R

All the Crossley-built bodies were on MCCW frames.
Withdrawn 1959 (1167-1168, 1171), 1960 (1169-1170).

1942

Fleet No.	Reg. No.	Chassis	Chassis No.	Body	Seating
1172-1174	GNA90-92	Crossley TDD4	92485-87	Crossley	H28/26R

All the Crossley-built bodies were on MCCW frames.
Withdrawn 1959 (1172-1173), 1960 (1174).

1943

Fleet No.	Reg. No.	Chassis	Chassis No.	Body	Seating
1175-1176	GNA93-94	Crossley TDD4	92488-49	Crossley	H28/26R

All the Crossley-built bodies were on MCCW frames.
Withdrawn 1959 (1175-1176).

Manchester Corporation Transport

Trolleybus Fleet List
1938-1966

Fleet No.	Reg. No.	Chassis	Chassis No.	Body	Seating

1949

Fleet No.	Reg. No.	Chassis	Chassis No.	Body	Seating
1200-1209	JVU707-716	Crossley Empire	944405/06/22/ 21/04/02/03/ 11/08/07	Crossley	H32/26R
1210-1219	JVU717-726	Crossley Empire	94419/20/09/ 13/18/10/14/ 15/12/25	Crossley	H32/26R

Withdrawn 1963 (1200-1219).

1950

Fleet No.	Reg. No.	Chassis	Chassis No.	Body	Seating
1220-1229	JVU727-736	Crossley Empire	94426/23/24/ 17/28/16/27/ 01/30/31	Crossley	H32/26R
1230-1237	JVU737-744	Crossley Empire	94429/33/32/ 34/36/35/ 37/38	Crossley	H32/26R

Withdrawn 1963 (1220-1237).

1951

Fleet No.	Reg. No.	Chassis	Chassis No.	Body	Seating
1240-1246	JVU745-751	Crossley Dominion	94503/07/04/ 02/05/09/08	Crossley	H36/30R
1247-1255	JVU752-760	Crossley Dominion	94501/10-12/ 06/14/13/ 15/16	Crossley	H32/26R

Withdrawn 1963 (1240-1255).

1955

Fleet No.	Reg. No.	Chassis	Chassis No.	Body	Seating
1301-1347	ONE701-747	BUT9612T	9612T185-231	Burlingham	H32/28R

Withdrawn 1962 (1346 [after accident]), 1964 (1305, 1307, 1309-1312, 1316-1317, 1319, 1323, 1326-1327, 1331, 1335, 1337-1340, 1344-1345, 1347), 1966 (1301-1304, 1306, 1308, 1313-1315, 1318, 1320-1322, 1324-1325, 1328-1330, 1332-1334, 1336, 1341-1343).

1956

Fleet No.	Reg. No.	Chassis	Chassis No.	Body	Seating
1348-1362	ONE748-762	BUT9612T	9612T232-46	Burlingham	H32/28R

Withdrawn 1964 (1351, 1355, 1358, 1360-1361), 1966 (1348-1350, 1352-1354, 1356-1357, 1359, 1362).

Acknowledgements

Without the pioneering work of the Manchester Transport Museum Society (and its predecessor the Manchester Transport Historical Collection), actively led by Cliff Taylor, it is extremely doubtful if this story could have been told. Their 1967 production on Manchester trolleybuses, long out of print, has, since publication, been an invaluable reference source and has settled many a family argument. A list of the Society's relevant publications is included in the bibliography, and the MTMS's permission to draw on these various works is gratefully acknowledged. The archive of the Greater Manchester Transport Society has equally provided a wealth of information and many photographs. Its Museum at Boyle Street, Manchester contains, within its collection, representatives of both fleets which are the main subject of this book. Geoff Hyde has readily made his study of Ashton-under-Lyne Corporation Transport available and Harry Postlethwaite has provided information based on his time at Hyde Road in the trolleybus era. Keith Hampton has provided a compendium of service development information, based on the work of Chris Boyes and others. Colin Reeve came to our rescue at a late stage to produce the system map. Eric Ogden has also been of considerable help, as have Elaine Altman, Peter Gould (with particular regard to fleet information) and Kevin Holland. Where conflicting information has arisen, giving rise to doubt about previously published facts, the 'official' version has been retained, pending further clarification.

Thanks are due to all the photographers, many of whom are, thankfully, still with us, despite the passage of four decades since the closure, for their work, and in many cases, for going beyond the call of duty to find those specific elusive views. In particular Stanley King, Peter Thompson and Geoff Lumb are thanked in this connection; in addition the latter has made available the fruits of his many years of research. Inevitably, my own modest collection of photographs, gradually enlarged and extended, mostly over forty years ago now, has been put to use, but regrettably not all of the prints provided the photographer's name, so for those whose pictures have had to be used anonymously, my sincere apologies. Individual attributions are shown below. My grateful thanks too, to my fellow members of the British trolleybus Society and the Sandtoft Transport Centre for keeping my interest in the trolleybus alive for so long.

Yet again, this work could not have been produced without the support and help of John and Mark Senior. The later was responsible for the concept; the former has diligently searched through not only his own collection of photographs, but also has combed through the archives at Pikes Lane, Boyle Street and Heaton Park over a period of years. This book is a tribute to his perseverance. Venture colleagues Scott Hellewell and Ian Stubbs have also rendered valuable assistance and support. As usual David and Mary Shaw have diligently proof-read the manuscript much to its benefit, but any errors or omissions that have crept in are entirely of my own making. Finally thanks are due to my daughter Catherine for ensuring I complied with the correct method of acknowledgement for referencing purposes, and for frequently reminding me to clean my glasses.

Individual Photographic Credits

GL	Geoff Lumb
GLC	Geoff Lumb collection
GMTS	Greater Manchester Transport Society
IY	Ian Yearsley
JAS	John Senior
JC	Jim Copland
JCG	John Gillham
JSK	Stanley King
NDC	Neil Dorsett collection
PT	Peter Thompson
RB	Roy Brook
RD	Ray Dunning
RGR	Bob Rowe
RGRC	Bob Rowe collection
RM	Roy Marshall
STA	Senior Transport Archive

Bibliography

The under mentioned sources have all proved helpful in producing this book, and if the reader has access to any of them, further study can be rewarding:-

Books

Yearsley, Ian: *Manchester Tramway Diary 1940-1951* (MTHC, 1961)

Eyre, Heaps and Taylor: *Manchester's Trolleybuses* (MTMS, 1967)

Hyde, WGS: *A History of Public Transport in Ashton-Under-Lyne* (MTMS, 1980)

Joyce, King and Newman: *British Trolleybus Systems* (Ian Allan, 1986)

Eyre, Michael and Heaps, Chris: *The Manchester Bus* (TPC, 1989)

Hyde, WGS and Ogden, E: SHMD Joint Board (TPC, 1990)

Keeley, Raymond: *Tramways In and Around Stockport* (Foxline Publishing, 1990)

Lumb, Geoff: *British Trolleybuses 1911-1972* (Ian Allan, 1995)

Eyre, Heaps and Townsin: *Crossley* (Oxford Publishing Co, 2002)

Ogden, E: *Lancashire United Centenary Celebration* (Venture Publications 2006)

Robertson SJT and Markham, JD: *The Regenerative Braking Story* (Venture Publications 2006)

Magazines

Tramway & Railway World

Electric Railway Bus & Tram Journal

Transport World

Passenger Transport

Bus & Coach

Buses Illustrated and Buses (Ian Allan)

Journals

Trolleybus (BTS)
Tramlink (TLRS)

Archive

The photographs, cuttings, and database on men of the transport industry held in the Senior Transport Archive at Pikes Lane have been invaluable for reference and also in providing material for illustrations

Websites

Peter Gould Local Transport History: www.petergould.co.uk/local_transport_history